# I KNEW DIETRICH BONHOEFFER

Dietrich Bonhoeffer

# I Knew
# Dietrich Bonhoeffer

EDITED BY
Wolf-Dieter Zimmermann
AND
Ronald Gregor Smith

TRANSLATED FROM THE GERMAN BY
Käthe Gregor Smith

*HARPER & ROW, PUBLISHERS*

*New York and Evanston*

First published by Christian Kaiser Verlag, München, under the title, *Begagnungen mit Dietrich Bonhoeffer: Ein Almanach*. Copyright © 1964 by Christian Kaiser Verlag.

I KNEW DIETRICH BONHOEFFER. Copyright © 1966 in the English translation by Wm. Collins, Sons & Co., Ltd., London, and Harper & Row, Publishers, Incorporated, New York. Printed in the United States of America. All rights reserved. No part of this book may be used or reproduced in any manner whatsoever without written permission except in the case of brief quotations embodied in critical articles and reviews. For information address Harper & Row, Publishers, Incorporated, 49 East 33rd Street, New York, N.Y. 10016.

FIRST EDITION

LIBRARY OF CONGRESS CATALOG CARD NUMBER: 67-11502

# Preface

This English edition of *Begegnungen mit Dietrich Bonhoeffer* varies somewhat from the German edition. The foreword by the German editor, Wolf-Dieter Zimmermann, has been replaced by this explanatory preface, by the foreword by Dr. Visser't Hooft, the General Secretary of the World Council of Churches, and by a brief outline of Dietrich Bonhoeffer's life. There is a slight abbreviation of Dr. Hammelsbeck's text, and the contributions by Ernst Wolf and Mrs. Bell have been replaced by two other pieces. These are the new essay by Professor Paul Lehmann of New York, which casts additional light upon Bonhoeffer's American visits, and the article by the late George Bell, then Bishop of Chichester. This recounts his meeting with Bonhoeffer in Sweden during the war. It is an important political statement, as well as the story of the last meeting between two friends. It first appeared in Bonhoeffer's *Gesammelte Schriften*, volume I, in 1958, and is reproduced here by kind permission of the publisher, Kaiser Verlag of Munich.

The intention behind these changes and additions is to make the story of Bonhoeffer's life more clearly available to many readers in the English-speaking world who wish to know more about this remarkable man.

In a volume of this kind the contributions, from family, and friends, and former students, are bound to vary greatly in style and in the impression they make. No attempt has been made to make them uniform, or to remove contradictions or slight repetitions. The motley effect is true to life. This is not a biography, but the raw material for approaching a personality who was by no means simple. If the critical reader notices even a certain incipient hagiography in some of the contributions,

# Preface

he will also be able to correct one impression with the help of another. The subject of all the essays nevertheless appears clearly enough through them, as a man who would have laughed to be described as extraordinary, far less as saintly.

A full biography of Dietrich Bonhoeffer is in course of preparation by his friend and heir, Eberhard Bethge. It will then be time for Bonhoeffer's contribution to contemporary thought to be fully assessed.

Meantime, here is a collection of quite personal impressions and accounts which both illumine the person of Bonhoeffer and fill in the background against which he worked and suffered.

*Ronald Gregor Smith*

# Contents

## I

## II

## III

## IV

# Contents

# V

# VI

# Illustrations

# Foreword

World wars build high walls between the generations. So the post-war generation shows little or no interest in the men and women who came to the foreground in the thirties and early forties. It is therefore all the more remarkable that Dietrich Bonhoeffer is an exception. Here was a young man whose life-work can only be understood in the context of the Hitler period, who was killed before the war was over and still he continues to speak. When the twentieth anniversary of his death is commemorated the large Kongresshalle in Berlin is filled with young people, his books are read in all parts of the world, he is quoted (and often misquoted) as a great authority.

There must be a reason for this. Is it not that a generation which has learned to suspect all the big talkers instinctively feels that Bonhoeffer is trustworthy? In his life conviction and decision are never separated. He is the least schizophrenic of men. It is for him a matter of course that once it becomes clear that National Socialism is a diabolical heresy he must give himself without reserve, without counting the risk, to the life and death struggle against Hitler.

But precisely because the man and the thought, his life and his books are so closely interwoven we want to find out all we can about him. This book containing personal reminiscences of his relations and friends brings us very close to him. We come to know a man of extraordinary openness to the world around him: literature, music, philosophy, politics all become part of his own life. But behind it all there is the man of faith who wants simply to be a loyal disciple of Christ and to whom it is given to have his faith tested and not found wanting.

A martyr? Bonhoeffer would not have liked such a big word for

what seemed to him such an obvious form of obedience. But
martyr originally means 'witness'. In that sense, certainly a
martyr.

*W. A. Visser't Hooft*

# Introduction

Dietrich Bonhoeffer was hanged at Flossenbürg in Bavaria on 9th April 1945. He was among the last of the thousands of victims claimed by the Nazis after the abortive attempt to assassinate Hitler on 20th July 1944. He has no grave – his ashes were scattered to the winds.

Among his fellow-sufferers was the élite of a whole generation in Germany. He was not an isolated figure.

Why then has he been singled out in the years since his death? Why do we concern ourselves with what this one man thought and did?

In a simple and easily understandable sense he stands for many. He stands for all in our time who act according to their conscience, who go against the stream, who will not submit to wrong. He was a man of simple and single-hearted courage. He was a witness to the truth. In all these respects many another man or woman might have become the symbol of resistance.

In a deeper sense Bonhoeffer has been singled out because he was both more self-conscious and more articulate than most of his fellow-sufferers. He was also more complicated. It is, I believe, the very ambiguities in his life and thought which have fascinated and stimulated both his immediate contemporaries and a whole new generation which never met him.

A brief outline of his life may be helpful for an attempt to come to grips with his personality and his ideas as they are refracted through the personal accounts given in this volume. He was born in Breslau in 1906, where his father was professor of neurology and psychiatry. He was brought up in Berlin, to which the family moved in 1912. On both his father's and his mother's side he came of families distinguished in German life.

# Introduction

It was a great liberal tradition which he inherited, and this liberalism extended deep into all his views, giving to his theology both breadth and humanity. He was a precocious student, and by the age of twenty-one he had completed a dissertation for his licentiate, *Sanctorum Communio*. In 1930 he was accepted as a teacher at the university of Berlin with a thesis entitled *Act and Being. Transcendental Philosophy and Ontology in Systematic Theology*. Thus he was launched on what looked like being a straightforward career in academic theology. There were intervals, as a young vicar to the German congregation in Barcelona, as a student at Union Theological Seminary, New York, and as pastor in London to two small German-speaking congregations.

But the rise of the Nazis to power in 1933 changed all that. Bonhoeffer was early associated with the church resistance to Hitler, which took shape as the 'Confessing Church'. He led a new seminary for ordinands in Finkenwalde in Pomerania. He went on teaching even after this seminary was officially suppressed in 1937. In turn he lost the right to teach at a university, the right to speak in public, and the right to publish.

By 1940 he was involved in illegal activities which aimed at the assassination of Hitler and the overthrow of the Nazi régime. This was basically consistent with his theology of involvement in the world. As he said later to a fellow-prisoner, 'If a drunken driver is at the wheel, it is not just the minister's job to comfort the relations of those he has killed, but if possible to seize the steering-wheel.'

So he became a courier of the Counter-Espionage Service which was led by Admiral Canaris. His official job was to exploit his ecumenical links for the sake of the German counter-intelligence system. His actual work was to further the conspiracy against Hitler. During this time he was able to journey abroad, especially to Switzerland and Sweden. It was on a visit to Sweden in 1942 that he carried to George Bell, Bishop of Chichester, proposals from the conspirators for peace terms with the Allies, in the event of a successful *coup d'état* in Germany. These negotiations came to nothing, as both Anthony Eden and Winston Churchill were opposed to any kind of negotiated peace.

On 5th April 1943 Bonhoeffer was arrested, and after two years in various prisons the end came. 'This is the end,' he whispered to a fellow-prisoner, the English officer Captain Payne Best. 'But for me it is the beginning of life.' He was thirty-nine years of age.

This is not the place to enlarge upon Bonhoeffer's original and revolutionary ideas, which range far beyond the normal scope of theology. In a forthcoming symposium, *World Come of Age*, his ideas are discussed at some length by many distinguished scholars.

One thing is certain. In the midst of the radical re-appraisal of traditional theology and traditional church patterns and structures, which is going on in every denomination today, Bonhoeffer's work – by which I mean not only his books and his letters and papers, but also his life as a witness to the truth – will continue to excite and focus attention.

R.G.S.

# I

1906    4th February, born in Breslau

1912    Father called to chair in Berlin University

1923    Begins theological studies in Tübingen

1924    Three months in Rome and North Africa; further studies in Berlin

1927    17th December, receives his licentiate of theology (the equivalent of a doctorate) with *Sanctorum Communio*, under the guidance of Seeberg

1928    17th January, first theological examination in Berlin; 15th February, begins his year as curate in Barcelona

1929–30    Assistant to W. Lütgert in Berlin

1930    8th July, second theological examination

18th July, 'habilitation' (acceptance as a university teacher) with *Act and Being*

31st July, inaugural lecture, 'The Question of Man in Modern Philosophy and Theology'

5th September, leaves for New York for a year's study at Union Theological Seminary

1931    Two weeks in July with Karl Barth in Bonn

# Childhood and Home
## SABINE LEIBHOLZ

My twin brother Dietrich was born ten minutes before me, on 4th February 1906, a proud advantage which he liked to stress when we were children. He was one of a large family of brothers and sisters: Karl-Friedrich, Walter, Klaus, Ursula, Christel and the eighth child, Susanne, who appeared three years after us. At that time our parents lived in a pleasant and spacious house at the Scheitniger Park in Breslau, where our father was a professor of psychiatry and neurology, and director of the hospital for nervous diseases.

My first memories go back to 1910. I can still see Dietrich in his little party dress, caressing the blue silk petticoat underneath; later, I see him beside our grandfather who, with baby Susanne on his lap, is sitting in front of a window through which the golden light of the afternoon sun is streaming. Here the lines of the picture dissolve, and the only other memory that comes to mind is of games in the garden during the sultry summer of 1911: Dietrich with a shock of flaxen hair framing his tanned face, hot from romping about and trying to ward off the midges, seeking shelter in the shady corner but reluctant to obey the nursemaid's summons to come in because he is still so wrapped up in his game and oblivious of heat and thirst. Our mother told us later that Dietrich had been an insatiable baby who roared when taken off her breast so that I could be fed; accordingly, it was arranged that I take precedence over Dietrich, who was then allowed to drink till he found out for himself that there was nothing left. After that he fell asleep. He loved his dolls, but later a stable and a knight's castle held more attraction for him.

Our mother had a strong personality. She was intelligent,

warm-hearted and unaffected, a good organizer and socially very gifted. At that time a governess, nursemaids, housemaids and chambermaids and a cook kept the big household running, and mother remained free and always ready for essential things. With her spontaneity she brought surprises, fun and parties into our nursery, and she was full of rhymes and songs. But she also introduced us to the serious side of life; she had taught our elder brothers and sisters herself for one or two years; there was even a schoolroom in the house with desks in it. Dietrich and I, however, were taught at home by Fräulein Käte Horn, as Mama was very busy; she only gave us religious instruction. She read to us or told us the Bible stories, always in the biblical text, and she opened the large picture Bible and explained the relevant picture. We loved this. With persistence and strictness she reproved us for futile excuses and cheating, but she had great understanding for all our nonsense and our interests. Our elder sisters got a room of their own set up as a dolls' house where they were allowed to do what they liked. The boys had a workshop on the ground floor, a carpenter's bench and a room for animals where squirrels and turtle-doves lived together in tall cages, snakes and lizards in a terrarium, and where they kept their collections of butterflies, beetles and birds' eggs. Nobody took it amiss when we tore our clothes at play or work, or broke things.

Our mother had a strong interest in and talent for teaching. At a time when girls mainly devoted themselves to their domestic and social duties, she had insisted on being trained as a teacher. She had probably inherited her artistic interests, her good taste, her talent for painting and her love of music from her mother, Klara von Hase, née Countess Kalckreuth. Grandmother had been a pupil of Klara Schumann and Liszt. Grandfather, a moderate and amiable man, was a son of the church historian Karl von Hase, and had been court preacher at the Garnisonkirche in Potsdam under Wilhelm II, but had fallen into disgrace when he criticized His Majesty to his face for speaking of the proletariat as *canaille*. As after that the Kaiser ceased to attend his sermons, he resigned and went to Breslau as a professor of theology. There my grandparents kept open house, and my mother met many interesting people. The background for this life was provided by wonderful antique furniture and the paintings of Lenbach, Achenbach, Schirmer, Feddersen, Voltz and many other artists, all of which came from the Kalckreuths.

Our father's ancestors had lived in Schwäbisch Hall since 1513, where some of them were given honourable burial in the Michaelskirche; they were goldsmiths, aldermen, theologians, later doctors and lawyers. From 1912 Father occupied the chair of neurology and psychiatry in Berlin and was the head of the university hospital. His most striking features were his eyes and the mobility of his expression. His head was well modelled, his hair and skin were dark. The movements of his finely built body were quick and lively. His extraordinarily beautiful hands were impressive too; his gestures were careful and balanced. He was rather distant and reserved, yet his eyes regarded the person in front of him with intense understanding. He would stress a point by preciseness, not loudness, of speech. He educated us by his example, by the way he lived his life. He spoke little, and we felt his judgement in a look of surprise, a teasing word and sometimes a slightly ironical smile. He had an unusually keen eye for what was genuine, spontaneous, creative. He showed his respect for warm-hearted, unselfish and disciplined actions and relied on us to stand by the weak. He hoped that we would learn to distinguish the essential from the inessential and to know our own limitations. His great tolerance excluded narrow-mindedness from our lives and widened our horizons. He took other people's goodness for granted and expected much of us, but we could always be certain of his kindness and his justice. He had a great sense of humour and knew how to tease us out of our inhibitions. His restrained temperament did not allow him to speak a single word to us which was not wholly concentrated on us. His rejection of the hollow phrase may have made us at times tongue-tied and uneasy, but as a result we could not abide any clichés, gossip, platitudes or pomposity when we grew up. Dietrich later realized this with gràtitude. Our father's love of nature was great. He was happiest in the forest. When on his walks he lovingly picked a plant and told us its name, it became alive for us, and we enjoyed finding one like it again.

Owing to Father's great talent for organizing his time, he was present at all meals, though he was immensely busy as head of the hospital, university professor and consultant. Ten minutes before each meal the gong sounded for us to wash our hands. We all assembled punctually round the big table which, by present standards, was almost a ceremonious affair.

Two housemaids served, and Fräulein Horn watched our manners and our plates. We had to finish the food which we had taken, a rule which Dietrich hardly ever found difficult. When the soup was served Mama asked: 'Whose turn is it to pray?' and one of us said: 'We thank you, Lord, for food and drink, Amen.' It was a rule never to discuss the food. Nor were we children allowed to speak at table, except to our parents, when we wished to tell them or ask them something. While the grown-ups were talking we had to be silent. Our father spoke in a low voice, and we listened all the more attentively. After lunch when our parents had their short siesta, or during surgery hours, it was not always easy for Fräulein Horn to keep us quiet. But this silence was insisted upon, for our parents thought it essential for our education that we should learn to consider other people. Sometimes our papa delighted in making us define concepts, or things, and if we managed to do so clearly, without being vague, he was happy. Occasionally he waltzed round the table with me, after the meal, and whistled the tune. He did not mention his work before us children. Once Dietrich discovered that patients were sent bills, and he preached his first sermon to my father, objecting to his accepting money from sick people.

Papa was cautious not to restrict us, if possible not to influence us; he was able to watch and wait for things to grow and did not want to tie us too closely to himself and others. And yet he was our ultimate authority. If our mother said: 'Father would not like that,' then this was enough. It was impossible not to notice our father entering the room. Very early Mama had impressed upon us the need to respect Papa's study, and it hardly needed the padded door to make us hesitate to knock; his desk was practically a sanctum for us.

In 1913 Dietrich started school at the Friedrichs-Werder Gymnasium, and this proved to be a difficulty as he was easily frightened and feared walking there alone, which involved crossing a long bridge. So he had to be taken at first, and his companion walked on the other side of the street so that he need not be ashamed in front of the other children. He eventually overcame this fear. He was also very frightened of Santa Claus, and he showed a certain fear of the water when we twins learned to swim. The first few times he raised a terrific outcry and had to be taken off the 'line' again. When he saw that I learnt more quickly than he and without tears, he probably felt more confident and overcame this fear. Later he was an excellent swimmer.

In spite of his exuberance and strength Dietrich was a sensitive child and did not attach himself easily to his schoolfellows. He found his playmates, of course, in his brothers and sisters. He and I shared a room between the ages of eight and ten, and at night in bed we had very solemn talks about death and eternal life. The 1914 war had broken out, and we heard of the deaths of our grown-up cousins, and the fathers of our schoolfellows. So, after the evening prayers and singing (which was always shared by our mother when she was at home), we lay awake a long time and tried to imagine what eternal life and being dead were like. We endeavoured every evening to get a little nearer to eternity by concentrating on the word 'eternity' and excluding any other thought. It seemed very long and gruesome, and after some time of intense concentration we often felt dizzy. For a long time we clung to this self-imposed exercise. We were very attached to one another and each wanted to be the last to say good night to the other; this went on endlessly and often we struggled out of our sleep to do so. I believed that this ritual saved Dietrich from being 'devoured' by Satan. We twins kept all this absolutely secret. Another exciting event for us children was the arrival of a refugee family from East Prussia in our house, to whom our mother gave two rooms.

I think that here Dietrich would want me to remember with gratitude Fräulein Horn who joined our family six weeks after we were born, to look after our three elder brothers. She came from the Herrnhuter Brotherhood, and we learnt even more hymns now from her. For all her starched collar, her heart was in the right place and she became my mother's right hand, staying in our home for seventeen years until she married. She has remained close to us to this day. The starched collar soon disappeared, and one morning she told my brothers: 'Boys, today we'll put on leather shorts.' Dietrich, I and Susanne were in the charge of her sister, Fräulein Käte, who was also our teacher for the first year. Dietrich loved her dearly. Of his own free will he assumed the role of her good spirit who helped and served her, and when her favourite dish was on the table he cried: 'I have had enough,' and forced her to eat his portion too. He told her: 'When I am grown up I shall marry you, then you will always be with us.' Of the hymns we learned, Dietrich specially liked: 'Where does the soul find its home, its rest', 'Oh wait, my soul', 'Jesus, still lead on', and 'Let me go . . .'. Dietrich called them 'red' hymns. There were also 'black' hymns like 'Praise to the Lord' and 'Now thank we all our God'. This too was a secret language between us. In the evening we were allowed to choose our hymns, and if we took too long our mother started to sing one, for she knew long successions of stanzas by heart. When the lights were extinguished the phosphorescent gleam of our glowing crosses comforted us, though their shape sometimes made us uneasy. When at the age of twelve Dietrich got a room of his own, we arranged that he should drum on the wall at night as a sign that Susi and I should 'think of God'. These monitory bangs happened regularly and became a habit, until Dietrich noticed that they sometimes roused us from our sleep; then he stopped them.

Our parents had a holiday house in the eastern Harz Mountains. Friedrichsbrunn was a second home for us children where we enjoyed all the delights of the hills and the forests. We were allowed to invite friends and cousins, and the very journey in two reserved compartments under the supervision of Fräulein Horn and her helpers was fun. In the large garden of Friedrichsbrunn we could do anything we liked. We scoured the glades, eagerly looking for mushrooms which we learnt to know well. Dietrich was beside himself with joy when he found a perfect specimen. I shall never forget Dietrich's sweetness of character which showed when we gathered berries on the hot summer slopes. He would fill my little pitcher with the raspberries he had toiled to collect, so that I would not have less than he, or share his drink with me.

On our journeys to the Harz Mountains Dietrich liked to stop over in Halberstadt and Quedlinburg to look at the cathedrals; in awe and admiration he stood and looked at them and investigated who was buried there. He knew a good deal of the history of those towns.

In the evenings the village children joined us in our big meadow for a game of ball. Dietrich liked to win at games, in fact he played with passion, but he was absolutely fair where others were tempted to cheat. Once he came home from a sports contest, crowned with a victor's wreath, but when his big brothers laughed at him for such ostentation, he took the wreath off with a blush. He was well and strongly built, and training at the horizontal bar had hardened his muscles; he liked me to feel and admire them. One day, in an exuberant

test of strength, he seized our bewildered Fräulein Lochstedt
and swung her on to the central-heating radiator.

At dusk we all sat in the living-room and played guessing
games or sang folk-songs, and watched the mists from the
meadows waft and rise along the fir-trees. When the moon
appeared, we remembered 'Oh look, the moon has risen' and
sang it. My father did not have electric light installed in this
house, perhaps so that we might be better able to watch the
coming of the dusk, the night and the stars. Paraffin lamps and
candles were brought in later. But we did have a telephone;
we took turns to tell our parents in Berlin what we were doing,
and they sometimes joined us for a few days.

Under the rowan-trees on our meadow Dietrich loved to sit
and read his favourite books, like *Rulaman*, the story of a man
of the stone age, and *Pinocchio* which made him roar with
laughter and whose funniest passages he read out to us again
and again. He was about ten years old at that time, but he
retained his sense of high-spirited comedy. The book *Heroes of
Everyday* moved him very much. They were stories of young
people who by their courage, presence of mind and selflessness
saved others' lives, and these stories often ended sadly. *Uncle
Tom's Cabin* kept him busy for a long time. Here in Friedrichsbrunn he also read the great classic poets for the first time, and
in the evenings we did play-reading with different parts. We
performed Hauff's profound fairy tale, *The Cold Heart*, which
he had dramatized in an amateurish way; he loved to act.
Once he played *The Imaginary Invalid*, later we even 'performed'
*The Journalists*. Our big dressing-up box with fairy and other
costumes was always a delight. Dietrich acted with complete
unselfconsciousness. When he felt that he gave pleasure to
others he did not think of himself. So even at the age of seventeen we two sang folk-songs together, when he held open house,
and accompanied ourselves on the lute in quite an amateurish
way; but obviously Dietrich's simplicity and feeling gave a
special effect to his songs. When at the age of eight he became

interested in music, our parents encouraged him to play the piano to us on Saturday nights. He soon became very good at sight-reading, and accompanied the cellos and violin, and the songs of his sisters. He loved to accompany our mother when she sang Gellert's psalms set to music by Beethoven, or, on Christmas Eve, the songs by Cornelius. Dietrich was a very sensitive accompanist; his goodness became evident here too in his attempt to cover up the mistakes of his partner and spare him humiliation before an audience. With truly touching patience he often accompanied us for hours and thus missed his own music practice. And yet he hoped for some time to become a musician, only he was critical enough to realize that he had not enough talent. First he played a great deal of Mozart and Beethoven, later more of Bach. We used all to go to the St. Matthew Passion in church, usually on Good Friday. But he also enjoyed romantic music very much. He loved the song 'Rest well', which the stream sings to the dead, so much so that he tried to transpose this Schubert theme into a trio.

At the age of thirteen we twins took dancing lessons, which were held in the houses of various families that my parents knew. Dietrich, still in shorts, looked on this as a kind of physical training, and had to be told more than once: 'Bonhoeffer, that is not a bow but a bend.' Still, he learned to dance well, preferring the open waltz, the quadrille, and the française which he danced gracefully. When he was eighteen, he even performed with me a very gay little play composed of songs and dances before a large audience, on the eve of our eldest sister's wedding.

Dietrich was a very chivalrous boy; he lifted the burdens off his sisters, pushed the book in front of me when we were reading from one together, though this made his own reading difficult, and was always kind and helpful if asked for anything. He loved the traditional festivities of our family. Here our mother was at her best. On the Sundays of Advent we all assembled with her round the long dinner-table to sing Christmas carols; Papa joined us too and read from the fairy tales of Andersen and Volkmann-Leander. The plate of sweetmeats and nuts went round while we were busy working at our Christmas presents. Dietrich liked carpentry but was sad that he had no talent for painting. He had not inherited the gifts for painting and sculpture from my mother's ancestors, the Kalckreuths and the Cauers.

Christmas Eve began with the Christmas story. The whole family sat in a circle, including the maids in their white aprons, all solemn and full of expectation, till our mother began to read. I shall always remember her like that in her black velvet dress with the lovely lace collar, her heavy brown tresses wound round her head, and under them her broad serious brow. She had the pale skin blue-eyed people sometimes have, but now she was flushed with the joy of the day. All traces of the fatigue and exhaustion caused by the Christmas preparations (which were extended far beyond our family) seemed to have vanished when Christmas Eve arrived. She read the Christmas story with a firm, full voice, and after that she always intoned the hymn 'This is the day that God has made.' I remember that sometimes tears were in her eyes when we sang the beautiful stanza: 'If I want to grasp such wonder, My spirit stands still with awe, It adores and understands, That God's love is infinite'; also when she read the words of the Christmas story: 'But Mary kept all these things, and pondered them in her heart.' Dietrich and I talked about this, it moved us very much and depressed us, and we were relieved to see Mama's eyes clear again. The lights were now extinguished and we sang Christmas carols in the dark, until our father, who had slipped out unnoticed, had lit the candles at the manger and the tree. Now the bell sounded, and we three small ones were allowed to go first into the Christmas room, to the candles at the tree, and there we stood and sang happily: 'The Christmas tree is the loveliest tree.' Only then did we look at our Christmas presents. When we were thirteen, Dietrich and I were allowed for the first time to stay up with the grown-ups on New Year's Eve. After a festive evening meal we first cast our fates in lead and then we played a family game of cards foretelling the future. About eleven o'clock the lights were extinguished, we drank hot punch, and the candles on the Christmas tree were lit once again. All this was a tradition in our family. Now that we were all sitting together, our mother read the ninetieth psalm: 'Lord, thou hast been our dwelling-place in all generations.' The candles grew shorter, and the shadows of the tree longer and longer, and while the year was fading out, we sang Paul Gerhardt's New Year's Eve hymn: 'Now let us go singing and praying, and stand before our Lord, who has given our life strength until now.' When the last stanza had died away, the church bells were already ringing in the new year.

In the war years 1916–17 Dietrich played at 'soldiers' in the garden with me, Susi and our neighbour's son. More drilling was done than shooting; but when a sand bomb was thrown against the hen run and a clucking hen burst forth, such war-like practice was considered mean by Dietrich and prohibited. 'Two against one is cowardly' was his martial law. It was touching how Dietrich saved his own sweets to give a surprise to others; he buried our sweet treasure in the garden, and later we gave parties and invited the grown-ups to share it with us. Our kind-hearted father even interrupted his surgery now and then and happily ate what we offered him. Dietrich was always very generous, and without anxiety or reproach he even lent his pocket-money to others. He also spent it in buying the most thoughtful presents.

The food scarcity in Berlin of 1917 and Dietrich's desire to relieve Mother of this care, perhaps also his own big appetite, roused unexpected qualities in him. He reconnoitred and reported about special rations, many times went to trouble to bring something home and was even perfectly informed about the food prices. I retain a lively memory of how such mercantile talents in Dietrich astonished and amused my father, for money matters were not talked about in front of us children.

In the spring of 1918 our brother Walter, at the age of eighteen, volunteered for the Western front as an ensign. Dietrich, then twelve years old, had on his own initiative practised the song: 'Now at the last, we say God speed on your journey,' and in the evening before Walter left, he sang it for him with great seriousness, accompanying himself. The next day we saw Walter off at the station. When the train started moving, my mother ran alongside calling out to Walter: 'It's only space that separates us,' and for a long time these words moved us deeply. A fortnight later Walter was killed on the Western front. Our mother's vital energy seemed broken; but helped by the loving-kindness of our father, and by her own strong and believing soul, she recovered. After a few years she arranged the most delightful parties for us again, and kept open house.

In 1922 we gave a fancy dress ball where Dietrich appeared dressed up as Cupid and let his blunt arrows fly without qualms. Such parties in our house enjoyed a certain fame; they never seemed to be boring. It may have been the mixture of artistic and academic traditions which lent such charm to our home and united in it so many people from the most different walks of life. The corner of the Grunewald where we lived could almost be called a professors' district. The Delbrücks, Harnacks and Hartwigs, the Plancks, His and Hildebrands lived there, and their young people as well as the young hospital doctors, musicians, theologians, lawyers arranged dances together and celebrated birthdays and successful examinations. Dietrich had inherited our mother's social talents and took great pleasure in entertaining people and making them feel at home.

When we were fourteen, we twins took confirmation classes with Pastor Priebe of the Grunewald Church. These classes were separate, but on Sundays we went to church together and sometimes talked the sermon over. Dietrich seemed to take an active interest in his class but hardly mentioned it. We were mainly instructed in a kind of moral theology. At that time

Dietrich began to wonder whether he should become a minister of religion. I remember he sometimes asked Fräulein Lochstedt to waken him earlier than usual, and when she came into his room in the mornings, he was often reading the Bible. One of the boys of his confirmation class whom Dietrich liked was Hans von Haeften. On 15th March 1921 we twins went together to church to be confirmed, which seemed more natural to Dietrich than to be with the other boys. Early in the morning our family had sung beautiful hymns for us before we got up.

Once when Booth came to Berlin for a great rally Dietrich was eager to take part in it. He was the youngest person there, but he was very interested. He was impressed by the joy he had seen on Booth's face, and he told us of the people carried away by Booth, and of the conversions. At that time he would have liked to be counted among the grown-ups. Once when asked how old he was he answered: 'Practically fourteen.'

After his school-leaving examination Dietrich asked me to go with him on a walking tour through the Thuringian forests, and again I experienced his sense of responsibility and care of others in quite a special way. Once, on the Inselberg, we got into very deep snow for which we were not prepared. My long skirt was flapping round my ankles heavy with encrusted ice, and we sank to our knees in the snow. Dietrich took my knapsack and carried it, he led me and stamped out a trail for me to walk in. Later we reached the Wartburg; he could hardly tear himself away from it. The wintry landscape lay spread out before us glittering in the sun. The Nicolauskirche in Eisenach roused his enthusiasm, also Bach's house. From the Kicklhahn we looked down 'over all the tree-tops'.

Dietrich's teachers at the Grunewald Gymnasium appreciated his open and considerate nature. His elder sister Christel went to the same school and wanted to study biology. Our parents desired to give us every possibility for full development, and our wishes were fulfilled when they sprang from genuine interests. Dietrich's inclination for theology became apparent when he was fourteen. He had never had any difficulty in learning, had sometimes brought prizes home and had obviously been the leading spirit of his form. His schoolfellows had liked him though he had never found an intimate friend among them.

But in those eventful times he was stimulated by his elder brothers. He shared artistic interests with Klaus, they often went to the Kaiser Friedrich Museum together, and to the concerts in the Philharmonie. Dietrich's philosophical interests began to awaken too, he discussed a lot with the brother who concentrated on natural science, and he listened to fierce political discussions. Karl-Friedrich had returned from the war. From Klaus, Dietrich heard of the fate of Russian emigrants and of the burning economic and social problems. He doubtless recognized the seriousness and urgency of all this. But it was only under the National Socialist régime that he became seriously concerned with politics. His heart and his mind searched for another way. When he had found it, these conversations often turned into passionate fights against the scepticism of the natural scientist, in spite of tolerance on both sides. He always met with sympathy for his unshakeable convictions, even when his decision to study theology was not really appreciated. At that time our mother often accompanied him to church. And of course it was in the family tradition that he should feel drawn to theology. This decision now heightened his energy, and he looked forward immensely to his first semester in Tübingen.

Our childhood was now over, and our paths diverged. Dietrich went to Tübingen for two semesters. To our horror he suffered severe concussion while skating. Tübingen had been the home of the Bonhoeffer grandparents after our grandfather had retired from the post of president of the county court. After his death our grandmother had joined us at the age of eighty-one. Her mind was as fresh as ever, and she was intensely alive to everything around her. When she died at the age of ninety-four, in 1936, Dietrich preached the funeral sermon.

In the early spring of 1924 Dietrich spent three wonderful

months in Rome and North Africa with Klaus, and I got engaged that year. Dietrich showed great affection to my fiancé, Gerhard Leibholz, and was always very close to him. In 1924, when I returned from a semester at the Art College in Breslau, Dietrich met me at the station in Berlin, and greeted me with a kiss. This gave me special delight, for it was not a custom among us brothers and sisters. He had brought me a beautiful old guitar from Rome, which he showed me with great pride. What a burden it must have been for him on the long journey.

Dietrich was warmly attached to every member of his family, yet sometimes he must have felt that the atmosphere was too narrow for his spirit. In the midst of the liveliest conversations, surrounded by his numerous family and friends, he was suddenly seized by melancholy. Then he slipped out unnoticed and sat somewhere by himself. Was he touched by a paroxysm of inner loneliness? Was it the 'eros of far-away'? He did know what homesickness meant. Did he foresee the dangers to his family? Otherwise he seemed so composed to us, so happy and harmonious.

He had already the gift of perfect assurance of manners; he listened attentively and attached great value to dealing politely with other people and keeping a certain distance – not from haughtiness, but from respect of the other's personality on which he did not want to impinge. He was disgusted with boorish and forward behaviour. At the same time, everybody felt his warm-heartedness; his big strong hand seized the hand of the other person so kindly. He always turned his gaze fully towards him to whom he was speaking; thus I still feel his hand grasping mine at our farewell, at the end of July 1939, at the station in London where I remained behind with my family. It was the last time.

# Professors' Children as Neighbours
## EMMI BONHOEFFER

My earliest memory of Dietrich Bonhoeffer is of his joining us three youngest Delbrück children at our ball game, which helped us to pass the terrible last half-hour before lunch in the hungry years of 1916–18. Dietrich was then about twelve, and he shook his head over the playing-ground we had chosen, the street, which he despised. But he joined us all the same. Dietrich, strong, blond and blue-eyed, resembled my brother Justus so much that my father on his lunch-time walk in the Wangenheim Strasse could not tell them apart, though Justus was his senior by almost four years. I was one year older than Dietrich, and the fourth partner was my brother Max, the same age as Dietrich, but much more delicate. We adored our big brother, Justus, because he was absolutely just and fair at our games. Dietrich seemed to fit in, and therefore he was accepted.

Soon we found out that Dietrich played the piano, his elder brother Klaus the cello, his sister Sabine the violin like myself, and that his other sisters had contralto and soprano voices and sang *lieder* by Schubert, Beethoven and Brahms. I forget how it started, but for years we played chamber music of a sort and went to the concert halls, all of us together, or in pairs.

While we were playing, Dietrich at the piano kept us all in order. I do not remember a moment when he did not know where each of us was. He never just played his own part: from the beginning he heard the whole of it. If the cello took a long time tuning beforehand, or between movements, he sank his head and did not betray the slightest impatience. He was courteous by nature.

Playing with others not only reveals one's musical talents but also one's character, and develops the ability to subordinate

oneself to the whole. For the pianist the alternation between leading and following, or the balancing of the two, is a very delicate matter, and his brother Klaus often pointed it out to him. Technically, Klaus was not as good as Dietrich, but he was his superior in musical sensitivity, and it was equally beautiful, in a musical and in a human sense, to see how Dietrich could sometimes be nothing but a listener.

In later years, we had our parties and dances where wit and imagination triumphed, and skating on the lakes till it was dark; both the brothers performed waltzes and figures on the ice with a simply entrancing elegance. Then, on summer evenings, we had strolls in the Grunewald, four or five couples of the Dohnanyis, the Delbrücks and the Bonhoeffers. Of course there was occasional gossip and vexation; but such things were quickly swept away: there was so much style, such a clear standard of taste, such an intense interest in different fields of knowledge, that this period of our youth now seems to me like a gift which at the same time carried an immense obligation, and probably we all felt that way more or less consciously.

Dietrich was in the habit, no matter whether he was in a hurry or not, of cutting street corners and taking the direct diagonal route, for instance when crossing the Kunz- and Buntschuh-Strassen. He walked with very straight knees, which made his gait look taut, almost rigid. He had inhibitions about greeting people he did not like, preferring to make a long detour. In greeting he lifted his round hat neither ostentatiously nor sloppily. His salute was always a real salute, a genuine and direct expression of his interest in the other person. But he was not conscious of these things, they were neither intentional nor a result of his education. He was like that, so his salute was like that. He showed the same intensity in playing music, or games, whether tennis, ping-pong, up-jenkins or boccia; he played to win, but was a good loser.

He had very strong hands; flabby hand-shaking was anathema to all of us, but even when he was a boy of fifteen to seventeen his grip on one's hand never hurt. To keep a distance in manners and spirit, without being cool, to be interested without curiosity – that was about his line. We liked to ask him questions that haunted us, e.g. was evil really overcome by good, or did Jesus want us to offer the other cheek to the insolent person too, and hundreds of other problems which drive young people into a deadlock when they face real life. He often countered with another question which took us further than a concise answer might have done, e.g. 'Do you think Jesus wanted anarchy? Did he not go into the temple with a whip to throw out the money-changers?' He himself was one who asked questions. He could not stand empty talk. He sensed unfailingly whether the other person meant what he said.

All the Bonhoeffers reacted with extreme sensitivity against every mannerism and affectation of thought; I think it was in their nature, and sharpened by their education. They were allergic to even the slightest touch of this, it made them intolerant, even unjust. Whereas we Delbrücks shrank from saying anything banal, the Bonhoeffers shrank from saying anything interesting for fear it might turn out to be not so interesting after all, and the inherent claim might be ironically smiled at. Such an ironical smile from their father may often have hurt the gentle natures, but it did sharpen the strong ones. My father took even the silliest questions of us children quite seriously and answered them objectively, so that we felt encouraged to ask. In the Bonhoeffer family one learnt to think before asking a question or making a remark. It was embarrassing to see their father raise his left eyebrow inquiringly. It was a relief when this was accompanied by a kindly smile, but absolutely devastating when his expression remained serious. But he never really wanted to devastate, and everybody knew it.

The house was run on a grand scale, which even in times of war and need was not restrained. The 'having as if one had not' permeated everything. In theory, one was liberal in tolerating other styles of living, but in practice the English 'that's not done' played so great a part that you felt it as soon as you were inside the porch. To wear a hat aslant was considered silly, to powder and paint one's face impossible. By such barriers the parents shielded their eight children from the threatening influence of the big city when they came from Breslau. Later on those barriers were of course lifted, but all the Bonhoeffers remained true to their kind, and who will blame them? The glass behind which the compass could vibrate was certainly clear.

Their mother was not that type of German *Hausfrau* whom Thielicke has called the 'blue-aproned categorical imperative'; she had too many servants to be that. But she was the lady of the house, she ran its social life, its cuisine, as well as the education, the games and the holidays of the children to perfection. Unforgettable are the summer weeks in the old forester's house at Friedrichsbrunn, which she had furnished quite simply with a cooking-range and cane furniture. There was no electric light. Each child was allowed to bring a friend, and all could play with the village children if they wanted to. What a paradise, compared to the boarding-houses in health resorts! Without any doubt the mother ruled the house, its spirit and its affairs, but she would never have arranged or organized anything which the father would not have wanted her to do, and which would not have pleased him. According to Kierkegaard, man belongs either to the moral or the artistic type. He did not know this house which formed a harmony of both.

Did his mother spoil Dietrich, who lived longer at home unmarried than the other children? She gave to each what they needed for their development and blossoming, giving them her warmth and her interest. Of course you can tell a person who comes from a home where the parents, regardless of themselves, have taken their duties very seriously. In a nursery, the delphinium grows taller and its flowers are a deeper blue than in the fields.

# An Oasis of Freedom
## FRANZ HILDEBRANDT

Bonhoeffer and I met in the seminar of Reinhold Seeberg on 16th December 1927, and on the next morning Dietrich defended his doctoral theses in the traditional public debate – the last requirement for obtaining the degree of a Licentiate of Theology. On that Friday night we found ourselves arguing, and we continued arguing through twelve years of unbroken friendship, till the outbreak of the war made contact between England and Germany impossible. But having talked theology with him (and indeed not only theology) meant that one could never talk like that to anyone else again, since he went. He was my senior in age and training by exactly three years; I did not know then how many years, how many dimensions, he was ahead of our whole generation. The sermons and essays of the pre-Hitler period which Eberhard Bethge has collected for us have made this abundantly clear. While we naïvely thought that all was more or less well with Church and State in the Weimar Republic, he had no illusions about the impending doom. The one thing that mattered in politics, while voting was still free, was to stem the Nazi tide; and when the worst had happened in 1933, Dietrich was ready for it. In the midst of the general capitulation on the part of the German intelligentsia the Bonhoeffer family, his parents, brothers, sisters and the old grandmother, stood with unclouded vision and unshaken will; their house in Berlin-Grunewald, soon my second home by adoption and grace, was an oasis of freedom, fresh air and good humour. The course for the Church was clear to him from the beginning and remained clear to the end; there could be no compromise with the brown hordes of Nazism and no patience with ecclesiastical diplomacy. We had attended each other's

ordination in the early 30's and had often toyed with the idea
of a joint pastorate in the East End of Berlin; and he could have
been appointed to a vacant charge in the summer of 1933, but,
in the biblical phrase, he was 'choosing rather to suffer affliction with the people of God'. He reasoned, in view of the so-
called 'Aryanization' of the clergy under the Nazi laws, that he
could not be in a ministry which had become a racial privilege.
I cannot recall or imagine any other man to have taken this line
of solidarity with those of us who had to resign their pastorates
under that legislation. Dietrich went to London in October 1933
as Pastor of the German Church in Sydenham, later destroyed
in the war and now rebuilt in his memory; I followed him for
two months as his guest into the parsonage at Manor Mount and
watched the beginnings of one book, treasured, perhaps, above
all others: *The Cost of Discipleship*. He was already in touch with
George Bell, the beloved Bishop of Chichester and patron of the
oppressed Christians and Jews in Germany, to whom he gave
me the first introduction; and I always found significance in
the fact that they shared the same birthday, 4th February –
a day which the contemporary Church can hardly afford to
forget. It was also through George Bell that I received the last
personal greeting from Dietrich after they had met in Stockholm
in 1942 where he informed the Bishop about the plans for the
overthrow of the Hitler régime; and again we were joined in
holding the memorial service for him in Holy Trinity, Kingsway,
in 1945. Of the ecumenical aspect of his work others will have
spoken; it would certainly have been sufficient reason to keep
Dietrich in London; but the ties with the Church militant at
home proved stronger, after all, and the return to Germany,
as head of the now illegal Seminary in Finkenwalde, was in-
evitable. Initially, in 1935 (I was then with Niemöller in Dahlem) we had some difficulty in pressing Dietrich to accept this
call; later, when he could have stayed with safety in America,
he chose, once again, to be with his suffering brothers and
students and in retrospect viewed these years in the cause of

underground ministerial training as the most fruitful period of his life. He was, after all, a born educator. But he was much more – in the words under his memorial in the Flossenbürg Church: 'Dietrich Bonhoeffer – a witness of Jesus Christ among his brethren.' I have already quoted from the eleventh chapter of Hebrews, and reading it further, three phrases about the first Christian martyrs strike me as I think of him: the fact that 'they were tortured, not accepting deliverance'; the verdict 'of whom the world was not worthy', and the promise that 'they without us should not be made perfect'.

# Paradox of Discipleship
## PAUL LEHMANN

Dietrich Bonhoeffer and I met for the first time in Union
Theological Seminary, New York. The time was late in September, as the academic year, 1930–31, was getting under way.
Bonhoeffer had come as the 'German Fellow' for that year. He
had been appointed to an exchange fellowship, granted an-
nually by the Seminary to selected students from various countries abroad. His advanced theological studies had already been
completed with the degree of Licentiate in Theology at the
University of Berlin. Thus he was free to pursue studies at
Union without the limitations imposed by a degree programme.
He was free also to explore and to absorb the *manière d'être* of
the United States on the threshold of the Franklin D. Roosevelt
era. The country was in the trough of a severe economic
collapse and in search of re-constructive leadership. With characteristic German thoroughness and passion, Bonhoeffer made
full use of this freedom.

The Philosophy of Religion, then under the remarkable mind
and spirit of Professor Eugene Lyman, was as distant as could
be from a German theological student whom the theology of
Karl Barth had begun to turn away from German Idealism towards Christian orthodoxy. If Lyman was at the centre of
Bonhoeffer's theological explorations, the Negro community in
Harlem was at the centre of his social exploration of the country to which he had just come. Here again, he focussed upon
what was most remote from his previous experience. His guide
in this area turned out to be a gifted Negro student at the
Seminary, Franklin Fisher. Those of us who shared Bonhoeffer's
theological and social concerns were often puzzled, and sometimes even amused, by these goings-on. We could understand,

and even share Bonhoeffer's interest in Lyman and Fisher. But why this absorbing fascination? How is it that, in retrospect, Lyman and Fisher acquire symbolic proportions in relation to Dietrich's American odyssey?

An answer to this question may be undertaken only with the greatest caution. Memory, especially when combined with respect, admiration and affection, may confuse reality with embellished impressions. After an interval of more than thirty years, moreover, it is not a little difficult to distinguish between the Bonhoeffer one first encountered and the Bonhoeffer one has reflected upon in the light of his own impact upon the period. Nevertheless, I should like to venture an answer to the question raised by Dietrich's American odyssey. It is an answer which seems intrinsically to connect the Bonhoeffer of my personal encounter with the Bonhoeffer of contemporary pre-occupation. Bonhoeffer exhibited in his life, already as a student, that which became increasingly evident in his writings, and in the death to which his labours led him. This was *the paradox of discipleship*. These signs or marks of this paradox may be briefly noted, all of them conspicuous during the year of our life together at Union Seminary.

First of all, Bonhoeffer was an 'un-German German'. Characteristically German were his blond hair and heel-clicking, head-nodding, stiffly bowing handshake. His impressive physique lent support to a resolute bearing and firmness of purpose that simply took command, uncalculated command, of every situation in which he was present. It was apparent that he was destined for leadership, for which he was equipped by national and cultural habit. Characteristically German also were the range and rigour of his knowledge, his impatience with mediocrity of thought and taste, and with anything less than the thoroughness of which excellence of achievement is born. In seminars, he was exasperated, not so much by the theological opinions of his fellow students, as by the shallowness of thought and knowledge out of which these opinions appeared to him to emerge. I shall always remember his refusal to play tennis with me after I had acknowledged that I had no expertness at the game. His view was that my incompetence was an obtrusive pre-emption of the court from those whose serious and practised playing of the game entitled them to it. The same unyielding demands, however, he made of himself. He was determined to learn to drive an automobile. At least three or four times (to his great exasperation) he failed the driver's performance test. He suspected, probably rightly, that his failure was due to his persistent refusal to place a five dollar bill at the disposal of his examiner. But persistence triumphed in the end. And in order to make assurance doubly sure, he urged me to accompany him and two mutual friends, Erwin Sutz and Jean Lasserre, on the first lap of his cross-country drive to Mexico City. By the time we had reached Chicago, Bonhoeffer was ready to operate the car to his own satisfaction and to the safety of the highways.

Characteristically 'un-German', however, were a noticeable absence of condescension in his dealings with his fellow students, whether in classroom or in dormitory. Characteristically 'un-German' also was his openness to every new experience. This was, perhaps, what most drew him to Lyman and Fisher, not only readily but eagerly. It would have been very 'German' of him to have dismissed William James and John Dewey out of hand, as the architects of American activism and optimism. Instead he applied his German rigour and determination to a mastery, particularly of William James, under Lyman's guidance. Fisher was the bearer to him of a strange new world of *Menschlichkeit*, of human naturalness and cultural deprivation, of a people in whom he sensed the integrity of unaffected creativity, born of a mysterious combination of suffering and humour. The Spirituals haunted him with a lingering fascination. Perhaps, the most 'un-German' thing about him was his sense of humour. He never took a theological argument with ultimate seriousness; and even the refusal of the tennis game, though firm, was tongue-in-cheek. It is at least edifying to wonder whether Fisher's friendship was a providential introduction to the mysterious bond between suffering and humour against the day of his own 'cost of discipleship'.

A second mark of the paradox of discipleship was the combination in Bonhoeffer of conservative and revolutionary passions and concerns. Aristocratic by heritage and taste, he could abandon luxury and even comfort for a longer claim upon him as a human being and as a Christian. His conservatism prevented a doctrinaire espousal of socialist theories and programmes of social change. On the other hand, his revolutionary sensitivity to the injustices of a colonial and capitalist society prevented an equally doctrinaire resistance to social change. His pacifism may have been rooted in an inbred Lutheran disquiet about the anarchy to which revolutionary social change is prone. If so, it was due no less to his unwillingness to accept life in this world as a mere 'holding operation' until the triumph of the spirit in the second coming of Christ. We spent much time during the second semester of that academic year patrolling the shipping offices in New York in search of a way of getting to India. Bonhoeffer was passionate about a visit to Gandhi, for reasons which were unclear to him at the time. Yet they seemed not unrelated to his search for a spiritual way of transcending the political and social polarities of western culture in transition. The trip never materialized. But Bonhoeffer's passion for it led him to disregard a substantial sum which his father had placed to his account in a New York bank and instead to accumulate some savings by dining several times a week at what were then a chain of restaurants, called 'The Coffee Pot', but better known as the 'Greasy Spoon'. It was a sign of the same capacity to suspend his aristocratic heritage and tastes and to identify with the victims of social injustice that informed his remarkable catechetical ministry in the slums of Berlin, in which he was engaged when I visited him there in 1933.

The third sign of the paradox of discipleship may be indicated by a phrase which Bonhoeffer himself was later to use in describing the life of discipleship. When he wrote of 'the hiddenness of the christian life', he didn't intend an autobiographical formulation. Nevertheless, the remark bears an unmistakable autobiographical stamp. The most significant recollection of the Bonhoeffer of my personal encounter is that he never allowed one to overlook the fact that he was a Christian, although he never wore his Christianity on his sleeve. His discipleship was at once open and hidden; self-committed and unself-conscious. To paraphrase a later formulation of his own, 'Jesus Christ was always taking form in him', without affectation, with conspicuous unobtrusiveness. To encounter Dietrich was, above all else, to encounter a person to whom humanity was natural. Utterly without obsequiousness, he was without a trace of status-seeking or of pretence, whether in meeting Seminary assignments, or in conversation, or in the inconspicuous adiaphora of dormitory living. Dietrich manifested a contagious freedom, openness and integrity in relating to all sorts and conditions of men, to people as *human* beings. This was the exact and concrete counterpart of his incisive and critical dealing with ideas. With people, he was as ready to listen as to speak, to identify as to analyse, to participate as to investigate. One did not notice the solitude which prepared him for fellowship, the discipline which sustained his abandon, the quiet piety which nourished the acumen of his lively mind. One did not notice because a rare and gentle, sometimes rebuking but always compassionate humour, carried and concealed a faith in daily triumph over doubt, a human spirit to whom nothing human was alien. Already as a student, Bonhoeffer was a 'man for others', taken captive by him whom he was later to celebrate as '*the* man for others'. He was a disciple of the humanity of Christ because in Jesus, the Christ, he had come to know the dead and resurrected God. It was the living God whose strength he found perfected in weakness; whose grace he attested as sufficient for every human condition; in whose service he found the freedom and the power to be truly and contagiously human.

# Friends

## EBERHARD BETHGE

Bonhoeffer could be very fastidious in the choice of friends, but once a friend, he was generous and many-sided. Sometimes he seemed imperious and demanding, but he also shared his money, his goods and his fate with those near him, unreservedly. How entertaining he was in tempting you to enjoy the culinary delights of foreign countries; how he taught you to rummage in antique shops with knowledge and zeal. He did not play off cinema against theatre or vice versa, but judged each in its own right. Before taking decisions about our enterprises, he was long in deliberating, too long; but once the decision was taken, it was neither regretted nor ever questioned. He was sharp in disputes, but could suddenly drop them. He took his friends seriously in their good and promising qualities, and quickly overlooked their bad ones. Only during the Church struggle did he abruptly break off friendships. But the friendships formed in Union Seminary lasted: he made four friends in the United States in 1930–31, two Americans and two Europeans, and they were to play an important part in his life.

The first of the two Europeans became his ally in dealing with the Sisyphean task of interpreting the theology of Old Europe in an American lecture-room. Erwin Sutz, a Swiss, knew where the wind was blowing from, and in what direction the arguments were aimed. Over and above that, a passion for playing the piano united them; they recommended each other to those people in New York who welcomed a musician in their house. Together they listened to Toscanini. Sutz was amazed that anybody was prepared to waste so much money on the post office and the Western Union to keep in touch with his family by

Dietrich and his twin sister Sabine

The Bonhoeffer's home in Marienburger Allee,
Berlin. Bonhoeffer was arrested in this house

telegram or telephone; there was a continuous dispatching of congratulations, an endless discussion of the problems of innumerable near and distant relatives. It was through Sutz's good offices that the overdue meeting between Bonhoeffer and Karl Barth was brought about. Sutz had been a student of Barth's and Brunner's. Bonhoeffer did not raise any critical questions about Barth's theology with his American fellow-students in 1930–31, but only with his friend Sutz, privately. So Sutz did not hesitate to introduce his new friend to Barth, and before his final return to Berlin Bonhoeffer spent a full two weeks in Bonn, where for the first time he met the man who more seriously than anyone else summoned him to theology. It was Sutz, too, who introduced him to Emil Brunner. During the war, Sutz became Bonhoeffer's important and reliable contact with the closed western world.

The other European was Jean Lasserre. At first Bonhoeffer did not consider him an ally at all. Here a Christian pacifist of his own age entered his own daily sphere for the first time. Moreover he was a Frenchman towards whom the German could not help feeling brimful of burning resentment. And lastly, he was a European theologian who could not be disposed of, like his American contemporaries, as being naïvely ignorant of the relevant history of dogma. In Lasserre Bonhoeffer met something different from the doubtlessly genuine seriousness of so many young theologians at Union: an obedience to Jesus's demand for peace such as he had never experienced before. Not that Bonhoeffer turned pacifist on principle, he never became one; but to be actively obedient to the biblical demand for peace, to take active steps against preparations for war – these were the lasting results of the meeting with Jean Lasserre, who made a deeper impression on Bonhoeffer than he realized at the time. It is he whom the passage about a 'saint' in the letters from the Tegel prison refers to, on the day after the plot of 20th July had failed.[1] It was he who struck the first spark for

[1] *Letters and Papers from Prison*, Fontana ed., p. 124.

Bonhoeffer's great book *The Cost of Discipleship*. The longing to feel divine grace active in his life, and the intellectual integrity not to reject its presence – these he shared with Jean Lasserre almost in amazement. Through this friend he awakened to the problem of how the sovereign Word of God was related to its bearer as a person and as the contemporary of his time and world. Soon Bonhoeffer found a fresh opening to the Sermon on the Mount. Soon, in urgent efforts, he drew his diffident friend to the ecumenical conferences which he had helped to bring about, so that the Frenchman's voice might be heard. Lasserre was present when Bonhoeffer gave his famous peace talk at Fanø, in 1934. In his addresses given in New York in 1930–31, Bonhoeffer had already stressed the biblical basis for peace, and the attempts for a peace movement in Germany (in the working-class and youth movement) in a way he had never done before.[2] This clearly shows that he was aware of the slight pacifist currents in Germany. But only when he met Lasserre, and the ecumenical idea entered his life, what had been a mere item of information changed him into a sympathizer with that movement, even identified him with it. The body of Christ was his biblical and ecumenical argument which he was to develop and consolidate in later years:

> You have brothers and sisters in our people and in every people, do not forget it. Whatever may happen, let us never forget that the people of God are a Christian people, that no nationalism, no hatred of race or class can perpetrate their designs if we are one.[3]

In 1953 Jean Lasserre argues on the basis of such thoughts (in his book *War and the Gospel*, published in Germany in 1956, p. 31):

> Nothing in the Gospel authorizes the Christian to destroy the body of Christ, no matter what he appeals to. Do we believe in the holy universal Church, the communion of

[2] *Gesammelte Schriften* I, pp. 66–74.
[3] *Gesammelte Schriften* I, p. 424.

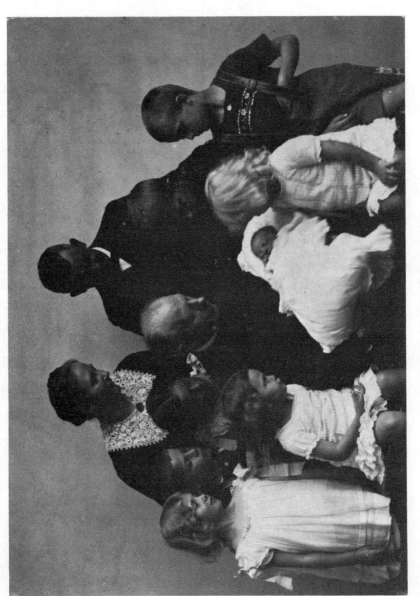

The Bonhoeffer family. Dietrich sitting beside the baby held by his uncle

saints? or do we believe in the eternal mission of France?
. . . We cannot be Christians and nationalists at once.
In 1930, such thoughts were unfamiliar to a German, and such
a conviction even rarer.

Bonhoeffer's relation to Frank Fisher, the third friend, whom
he also met in the lecture-room, was intensified and stabilized
by their daily and weekly programmes in Harlem. Fisher was
a slender Negro with a striking head. Bonhoeffer's friendship
with him did not have the spontaneous lightness that his
relation to Paul Lehmann had, but needed to be continually
confirmed in its freedom. But Dietrich Bonhoeffer was convincing, almost an artist in offering himself as an unprejudiced
partner. Once the friends had ordered a table in a good
restaurant; when it was indicated that Fisher would not be
served like everybody else, Bonhoeffer ostentatiously left the
place. When we remember the delicate relationship between
black and white in the United States, we must marvel at the
depth to which Bonhoeffer penetrated the intimate sphere of
the Harlem outcasts: he had the gift of restoring his native
pride to the sensitive and easily hurt person.

What was so impressive was the way in which he [Bon-
hoeffer] pursued the understanding of the problem to its
minute details through books and countless visits to Harlem,
through participation in Negro youth work, but even more
through a remarkable kind of identity with the Negro
community so that he was received there as though he
had never been an outsider at all.[4]

The experiences he had with and through Frank Fisher played
a major part in what Bonhoeffer later had to say of the U.S.A.
He never met him again, as he did the three others; Fisher died
in 1960 as a professor in Atlanta, Georgia.

It was Paul Lehmann, lastly, and his wife, who made the
United States a place for Bonhoeffer to which he was tied with
strong human links. He celebrated his twenty-fifth birthday

[4] Paul Lehmann, BBC talk, 13th March 1960.

with them. With Lehmann Bonhoeffer was able to chat, to dispute; he understood the finest nuances in culture, in taste, and in theology. Coming from the Evangelical and Reformed Church (later he joined the Presbyterians), he worked at Union Seminary for his thesis and was an assistant in the department of Systematic Theology. He knew why Bonhoeffer's hair stood on end when professors and students made 'theological' pronouncements: how impossible! Lehmann always hoped that one day Bonhoeffer might contribute to shaking the American 'theistic scenery' as it then existed. Thus it was he who did his utmost in 1939 to keep his friend in the country and save him. Lehmann found Bonhoeffer unmistakably German not only in his thorough theological training and his methodical exactness in tackling problems, but 'he was German in his passion for perfection, whether of manners, or performance, or of all that is connoted by the word *Kultur*. Here, in short, was an aristocracy of the spirit at its best.'

But he also thought him the most un-German of Germans. His aristocracy was unmistakable, yet not obtrusive, chiefly, I think, owing to his boundless curiosity about every new environment in which he found himself and to his irresistible and unfailing sense of humour. Thus he could suggest without offence that we should not play tennis together since he commanded a certain expertness at the game which I could not claim. . . . This curiosity about the new and different, this unfailing humour . . . always turned the incongruity between human aspiration and human failing away from human hurt to the enrichment of comradeship . . . the capacity to see oneself and the world from a perspective other than one's own. This paradox of birth and nationality in Bonhoeffer has seemed to me increasingly during the years since, to have made him an exciting and conspicuous example of the triumph over parochialism of every kind.[5]

[5] Paul Lehmann, BBC talk.

Union Theological Seminary, New York, 1930/31

1. Prof. Fleming 2. Prof. Scott 3. Prof. H. F. Ward 4. Prof. Reinhold Niebuhr
5. President H. S. Coffin 6. Prof. John Baillie 7. Prof. Julius Bewer
8. Prof. James Moffatt 9. Frank Fisher 10. Paul Lehmann 11. Erwin Sutz
12. Dietrich Bonhoeffer

## Friends

In patiently complying with every demand of his good friend in 1939 to invite him and then to cancel his invitation, which brought him into disrepute with his colleagues and the American colleges, and by accepting the fruitlessness of all his labours with the greatest, though sorrowful, understanding, Paul Lehmann became the instrument and partner of Bonhoeffer at the most crucial turning-point of his life.

# II

1931 From 1st August, lecturer in the theological faculty of Berlin University

1st–5th September, conference of the World Alliance at Cambridge, nominated secretary of the Youth Group

From 1st October, chaplain at the Technical College, Berlin

15th November, Ordination

During the winter semester 1931–32, lectures on 'The History of Systematic Theology in the 20th Century'

From November 1931 to March 1932, holds a confirmation class in Berlin-Wedding

1932 During the summer semester lectures on 'The Nature of the Church'

26th July in Cernohorske Kupele (Czechoslovakia), giving a paper on 'Towards a Theological Establishment of the Work of the World Alliance'

In August, takes part in ecumenical conferences in Geneva and Gland

During the winter semester 1932–33, lectures on 'Creation and Sin' and 'Modern Theological Literature'

1933 1st February, radio talk: 'Changes in the Concept of the Leader Principle'

In April, essay: 'The Church and the Jewish Problem'

During the summer semester lectures on 'Christology', also a seminar on Hegel's Philosophy of Religion

In August, co-operation at the 'Bethel Confession'

7th September, preliminary work with Martin Niemöller, for the Pastors' Emergency League

15th–20th September, takes part in the conference of the World Alliance in Sofia

27th September, in Wittenberg, distributing protest leaflets of the Pastors' Emergency League at the beginning of the National Synod

# At Zion Church

## FRITZ FIGUR

One day a baker, Herr H. of the Oderberg Strasse, appeared in my house. He said he had a furnished room to let, and somebody had inquired about it, a curate of the Municipal Synod called Bonhoeffer. Did I think he was a Catholic? I reassured him that Bonhoeffer was by no means a Catholic, and so Dietrich went to live in the Oderberg Strasse of Berlin N.58, which is situated between the Alexander Platz and the Old 'Exer' – not in Moabit, as has sometimes been said. At that time he held the important post of a curate of the Municipal Synod, i.e. assistant preacher at the Zion Church, with a monthly salary of 420 marks [now approximately £40.] He had not been able to find lodgings in his own parish. As in Berlin the streets of the different parishes merge into one another, he had thus complied with his duty to reside near his own parish, though 400 yards away, within the neighbouring parish of the Segenskirche, my own parish.

Thus I often met him, with or without our mutual friend Franz Hildebrandt of Dahlem. He preached simply, using little known texts and good metaphors. To follow a series of successive texts had not become a fashion again at that time, and we young pastors vied with one another in discovering unknown texts. Once when he met me in the street and asked me 'What are we to preach about on Sunday?' I named a passage which surprised him very much. His language in his dissertation for the licentiate was so difficult that even Reinhold Seeberg groaned over it; but everybody could understand his sermons. I did not often hear him preach but I still remember his texts and his metaphors.

The young people understood him too, his confirmation

class was devoted to him. His room in the Oderberg Strasse was often full of them in the afternoons. Not everybody has had the fun of seeing him cutting up a bale of cloth, which he had probably purchased cheap, for confirmation suits for those boys. I remember from that time some conversations with him about infant baptism. As a young pastor I was worrying about the habit of mass baptisms. Later, after his time as an assistant preacher, with the Church struggle approaching, there were reflections about the relation of the Confessing Church to Catholicism. Was he a 'Catholic', after all?

As students we only met in one lecture, about organ theory and campanology, where our study books had to be signed, as attendance was compulsory for the examination. Most of us wasted our time on trivialities during these lectures, or wrote letters; but Bonhoeffer learnt Hebrew. Such zeal impressed me enormously.

Though I was bombed out during the war and my belongings were stored away, I have kept a fine souvenir from the time when Bonhoeffer was assistant preacher at Zion and we were neighbours. He and Hildebrandt had published a Lutheran catechism with the title 'If you believe, you have it'. One copy was dedicated to me. Bonhoeffer wrote in it: 'To my present pastor'; Hildebrandt's inscription is a little more ironical. Bonhoeffer was himself a pastor to an eminent degree. The traces of his unfinished life and work are widely scattered. One of the first important items of news which was secretly received on one of the few radio sets left in a small Brandenburg town, after the defeat, told of Bonhoeffer's death. I heard this when I arrived there after a short period of imprisonment. How much more he would have had to say! Fragments, scattered pieces, new beginnings – in reference and gratitude we hold in our hands what he left behind. So often God works with broken tools and builds his Church even in a religionless world.

# A Confirmation Class in Wedding
## RICHARD ROTHER

Dietrich Bonhoeffer was our confirmation pastor in 1931. Perhaps we were the only group he ever prepared for confirmation – forty boys from the north of Berlin who belonged to the parish of Zion Church. Superintendent Müller, who had looked after us, died and left our class without a pastor, and that is how we got Dietrich Bonhoeffer, who prepared us for our confirmation in a politically stormy time, in the spring of 1932.

On the same Sunday the elections took place and everywhere in the north of Berlin political tensions were high. But Pastor Bonhoeffer was beloved and respected by his congregation and the confirmation ceremonies suffered no disturbances. Never before or after has Zion Church had such a strong congregation as when this gifted man was its pastor.

Our class, then, was fortunate to have such a man as its teacher. What do boys of that age normally care about the greatness of a man? But we may have felt something of it even then. He was so composed that it was easy for him to guide us; he made us familiar with the catechism in quite a new way, making it alive for us by telling us of many personal experiences. Our class was hardly ever restless, because all of us were keen to have enough time to hear what he had to say to us. Once one of us boys unpacked his sandwiches in the middle of the class and started eating. This was nothing unusual in the north of Berlin. Pastor Bonhoeffer said nothing at first. Then he looked at him, calmly and kindly, but long and intensely, without saying a word. In embarrassment, the boy put his sandwich away. The attempt to annoy our pastor had come to nothing through his composure and kindness – and perhaps through his understanding for boyish tomfoolery. To be near us, our pastor rented a furnished room in the north of Berlin. His landlady was explicitly instructed by him to allow us into his room in his absence – an expression of great confidence such as we had hardly experienced before, but which we certainly appreciated. He taught English to some of us in his spare time.

After we left school Pastor Bonhoeffer took ten of us to the Harz Mountains, where we spent a fortnight with him, an unforgettable time. For most of us this was the first journey away from the grey houses of northern Berlin. At that time of unemployment, in 1932, practically none of us had any money and there was no chance for a child to get away from the stony desert of the city. Bonhoeffer's original plan had been a journey to the Holy Land; but he put his personal wishes aside and later rented a piece of land in beautiful surroundings in Biesenthal near Bernau, in northern Berlin, where he had a week-end cottage built for us and for his students.

I remember one incident from our confirmation time very clearly. One of us boys was dangerously ill. In spite of many other engagements Pastor Dietrich Bonhoeffer visited him in the university hospital two or three times a week. Before the operation, he stayed with the boy to pray with him and to ask God to help him through those heavy hours. As it turned out, the boy's leg had not to be amputated after all; it was saved by the operation, and he made a complete recovery. On his confirmation Pastor Bonhoeffer gave him the text: 'God is love, and he who abides in love abides in God, and God abides in him.'

In the course of time, we forty confirmands from the slums of Berlin were scattered to the four winds. We were shocked and deeply moved to hear that our pastor had to die a cruel death as a martyr in the discipleship of Jesus Christ in April 1945. The gratitude which I feel for having had such a pastor in our confirmation class makes me write down these recollections.

# Years in Berlin

## WOLF-DIETER ZIMMERMANN

I studied theology because I came from a parsonage. But for two years I could not make head or tail of my studies. I subscribed to lectures in almost all faculties, to labour rights with Dersch, sociology with Vierkant, history with Hoeltzsch, Kant with Spranger and so on *ad infinitum*, for Berlin offered much in such fields. What I heard in theology bored me infinitely. The pedantic juggling with Greek words and theological concepts seemed meaningless to me, and gave me no guidance. For Reinhold Seeberg we had to translate texts from the late middle ages, but what they meant, how they were related to God's actions, I never discovered. The same was true of Sellin's formalistic dealing with the book of Isaiah, and of Deissmann's elucidation of the New Testament. Only Lietzmann in his introduction to the New Testament and his exegesis of the Synoptic Gospels gave us a picture of what had happened at the time of Jesus, and its meaning for us.

My 'studies' really took place outside the university. At that time I got acquainted with the Eckart Circle, and especially with Ernst von Salomon, the assassin of Rathenau, and Count Stenbock-Fermor, an active agent of the communists. With them I spent whole nights in discussions. Ernst Wiechert, Frank Thiess and Edzard Schaper read from their works in this circle, and some of us spent an hour or two with them after such readings. My evenings were filled with invitations, dances, and lectures, also with discussions with the group round Hans Schwarz, the editor of Moeller van den Bruck, and the members of the German Hochschulring (Universities' Association) like Schwarz van Berk, Harald Laceur, Otto Koffka, Bodenstein and Schinkel. Here I felt, though in a different form, something

I had learnt from Ewald von Kleist in Schmenzin, where I had first met that type of conservative. Hans Schwarz, who joined us for discussions once a week, drew my attention to Ernst Barlach; he once described to us in detail the production of *The Blue Boll* in the Staatstheater. Schwarz was a bachelor; his bedroom was papered in black; his flat was only open to the elect, to which Wolfgang Dibelius also belonged.

All this constitutes the background to the meeting which – with almost magnetic force – was to pull the strands of this chaotic muddle in one direction. It happened in the autumn of 1932. Once again I planned my studies for the coming semester, noted down the main classes and looked for some others that might be promising. Among them was a lecture on the Nature of the Church. When I entered the lecture-room, there were about ten to fifteen students, a disheartening sight. For a moment I wondered whether I should retreat, but I stayed out of curiosity. A young lecturer stepped to the rostrum with a light, quick step, a man with very fair, rather thin hair, a broad face, rimless glasses with a golden bridge. After a few words of welcome he explained the meaning and structure of the lecture, in a firm, slightly throaty way of speaking. Then he opened his manuscript and started on his lecture. He pointed out that nowadays we often ask ourselves whether we still need the Church, whether we still need God. But this question, he said, is wrong. We are the ones who are questioned. The Church exists and God exists, and we are asked whether we are willing to be of service, for God needs us. What fascinated me in this man from the very beginning was the way he saw things; he 'turned them round', away from where they were stored for everyday use, to the place God had ordained for them. And in the process the values which had been so familiar and natural to us were transformed as if by themselves. To tell the genuine from the unreal question was of the greatest importance for theology. I should have liked to write the whole lecture down, word for word. Every sentence went home; here was a concern for what troubled me, and indeed all of us young people, what we asked and wanted to know. There was a lot of systematic theology in this lecture, as well as dogmatics and symbolics; but they served as occasions for dealing with the main question. And this was: What has God done? Where is he? How does he meet us and what does he expect from us? To answer these questions, the doctrine of the Church was necessary; it had no meaning in itself, it·was part of the explanation of how God became man, and saved man.

It followed as a matter of course that those few students, at least some of them, got in closer touch with Bonhoeffer. Thus it happened that Bonhoeffer suggested we should meet in the next semester, as a small group, outside the ordinary lecture. Not at his own home, however; perhaps he wanted to save his parents and their domestic set-up the trouble, or perhaps he did not want us to come so suddenly into contact with the middle-class aristocracy of Berlin. But as far as I remember he said something like being afraid to be thought too importunate or intimidating by the students. So we agreed that this group should meet in my room, once a week. I lived near the Alexander Platz at the Königstor, Berlin N.E. There were the parsonage and office of the superintendent, my father, and high up in the attics a small room with a bed, a washstand, desk, armchair and bookshelf – my room. Here ten to fifteen people met for discussion, sitting on every possible piece of furniture, always for about three hours. The air was thick with heavy smoking. Of the subjects we discussed I only remember one: What is a sacrament and what does it effect? The subjects themselves were not so important, I think. What was far more important for us was to find straight ways of thinking and to learn not to slink off into side-issues, or to be satisfied with premature cheap answers. That winter 1932–33 did not produce anything, but it taught all of us to 'theologize'. We were also able to speak to one another about political developments and the crisis in the Church, but only, as it were, peripherally.

# I Knew Dietrich Bonhoeffer

These discussion evenings consisted in pure, abstract theorizing, in the attempt to grasp a problem in its fullness, and to examine and test the possibilities of answering it. Topical problems were dealt with later, from about 10.30 on, in a beer cellar at the Alexander Platz. Every evening meeting ended that way, and always we were his guests. Work and pleasure, objective discussion and heart-to-heart talk, everything had its proper place. This was the only experiment of the kind that Bonhoeffer made. Then the Church struggle began, and more students attended his lectures and seminars. It became more of a university activity; crowded lecture-rooms, open evenings with fifty to sixty students; the former intensity could not possibly be maintained.

In the lecture-room Bonhoeffer was very concentrated, quite unsentimental, almost dispassionate, clear as crystal, with a certain rational coldness, like a reporter. It was the same with his sermons. He never had full churches, as far as I can judge. When he preached in the Trinity Church during the semester, there might be sixty to seventy people sitting scattered and forlorn in the spacious church. Even though his lectures were well attended, his services remained almost unnoticed. I was very impressed by his sermons; but perhaps only a certain type of person responded to them. The average Berlin congregation could not make much of what he had to say, nor indeed the clergy, at least not those in my father's diocese.

Probably Bonhoeffer was always an outsider, not only for the students, but also for the professors. Many of his colleagues at the university hardly remember him now, and the same is true of many men in the administration and direction of the Church. He was a theologian of the new generation, and just starting. Others were more important, more distinguished, more influential. The Church struggle thoroughly destroyed these perspectives, producing new structures in the universities and the churches.

In 1933 the Church elections took place, and the result was

that the National Socialist ideology penetrated the realm of the Church. From that time we spoke of certain Church areas as being 'destroyed', namely those provinces whose ecclesiastical administration was seized by the Nazis. Shortly before that, there was an election meeting in the Auditorium Maximum of the University. It was crowded. There were sharp and aggressive speeches from one side, there was moderation couched in civilized terms, and almost ineffectual, from the professors' side. Then Bonhoeffer stood up and started speaking with the words: 'If God leads his Church into battle, he wants to tell her something by that.' And he went on to explain the task the Church was called upon by God to fulfil today. On the whole this speech hardly persuaded anybody who was not already thinking along those lines; but to some of us it gave exactly the answer we had waited for. At that time an election manifesto appeared from the Young Reformation Movement, which maintained that the Confessing Church should be unpolitical. Bonhoeffer read it in fury: 'Here the Church capitulates before politics.'

In March of that spring Klaus Bock and I went with him to his shack near Bernau: he had invited us for a few days. Fortunately we had mostly sunny weather, for the place was not what we had imagined a week-end cottage to be like. It was a wooden shed, dusty inside after the winter, the furniture stored in a heap. We had first to clean up, put things in their place and make it habitable. It was very cold, with only a paraffin stove to heat it, and hardly more in it than three bedsteads, a few stools, a table. We were extremely surprised that Bonhoeffer was content with this primitive accommodation. Each of us was given certain duties, and in our spare time we two went for walks or sat in the sun at the edge of the forest. Bonhoeffer read books on Christology, he kept groaning: 'Oh, it is difficult.' He read with complete abandon and was, as often during such phases of work, quite absorbed by it. One evening we were sitting on the bank of a lake. Opposite, the setting sun was mirrored in the water; we were in raptures, and pointed it out to Bonhoeffer. He looked up for a second, looked across the lake, said: 'Imposing', and went on reading. Another time he surprised us by his knowledge of the constellations.

He had announced a lecture on modern theological literature. He planned to give a résumé of the books and an appraisal. For he knew that most of us had not read the great theological works and needed guidance to deal with the material. During the first lecture he asked whether there were requests for specific books. Somebody suggested Elert's *Morphology of Lutheranism*. Bonhoeffer answered: 'I know too little about it; I cannot discuss it.' In the second lecture he gave a brilliant paper about books in general, about their covers and their colours, about prefaces and lists of contents, about books with and without a definite structure, with and without illustrations, and about different types of print. For forty-five minutes we heard nothing but spirited and witty observations about books and their authors, about the right and the wrong way to deal with them. Nothing of theology and philosophy, only aesthetics and *esprit*. It delighted him for once to dissect books, in a medical sort of way.

On one of the open evenings he played records of Negro spirituals. It was for us an entirely unknown, strange and frightening world. He told us of his coloured friend with whom he had travelled through the States; how hotels and restaurants had refused admittance even to him as a white man when he was accompanied by his black friend. He told of the piety of the Negroes, their worship and their theology. There, he thought, was a Christianity in reformation. The official religion, however, was a kind of family affair, was club life and a 'social event' rather than a confession of faith. He spoke of themes for sermons, expositions of sermons. And he played the spirituals, translated them, explained them, interpreted them. A strange new world was beckoning to us. At the end of the evening he said: 'When I took leave of my black friend, he said to me: "Make our sufferings known in Germany, tell them what is happening to us, and show them what we are like." I wanted to fulfil this obligation tonight.'

Some more reminiscences from that time:

In his seminar, we discussed Hegel's philosophy of religion. Each of us had to give a paper on a specific theme. During one of the last sessions, someone quoted a passage from Hegel in his paper which according to him showed clearly that Hegel was here thinking along non-Christian lines. Proudly the speaker concluded that Hegel's *Philosophy of Religion* was not a truly Christian book. Bonhoeffer's answer to this was: 'An author should not be attacked or interpreted from one of his negative sentences; we should ask what he intends to say with the whole book.'

Once after a service the two of us walked across the Potsdamer Platz. We spoke about the sermon and then about himself. I explained to him that he often made an impression of coldness, of distance, that sometimes one felt almost repulsed by him, or as if he wanted to withdraw from the other person. Bonhoeffer stopped short and looking me full in the face asked: 'Why can't you let somebody be as he is?'

During another walk I said to him in perplexity, 'Praying seems to be rather a difficult matter; I do not know how to go about it, I suppose I shall never manage it properly.' He answered: 'Our prayers are always imperfect; but our prayers do not matter so much, for our praying only lives from the praying of Jesus Christ.'

Once, while talking of books, I asked him whether he owned a certain book: 'Yes, you can have it.' I refused, protesting in alarm, because I dared not carry off a book from a professor, whereupon he said: 'What on earth is your idea of property?' Somewhere in the north of Berlin, in Wedding, he ran a group of difficult boys whom nobody had so far been able to manage. To those boys he gave himself with the utmost devotion. Once he arrived fifteen or twenty minutes late for a seminar. It had never happened before, for he was always very reliable and correct. We looked at him in astonishment, but he only said: 'One of my boys is dying, and I wanted to have a last word with him. It had to be.'

Bonhoeffer was generous with money. He wanted to enjoy what gave him pleasure. He loved the theatre and cinema, music, good food and drink, travel and fashionable clothes. He wanted others to share these things too, he did not want to enjoy them in secret. Thus it happened that we once talked about money and property. He said: 'I only want to have so much money that I don't need to economize. Anyone who has more falls into temptation. Money must not become a power in life.'

A *Festschrift* was being prepared for Karl Barth's fiftieth birthday. He had not been asked for a contribution. Admittedly he was not a pupil of Barth's, but he had busied himself intensively with Barth's views, and had sought personal contact with him – as, indeed, he always did with the theologians who meant something to him: 'One must see and talk to people in order not to misunderstand them.' Consequently, he also felt very close to Barth, and he was all the more saddened by being excluded in this way. 'Oh well, it is after all quite good that I am not in it. I do not want to be branded as a Barthian, for I'm not one.'

When the Church struggle grew more intense and his life as a university teacher became more and more precarious, Bonhoeffer thought that now was the time to work in a congregation. There, he said, the great decisions will be taken, there is the Church now, the Confessing Church. In my father's parish of St. Bartholomäus there was a vacancy, and he applied for it. He preached about the stilling of the storm, about the anxiety of the disciples in their boat, and how they were changed, became other people, how they forgot and despaired. It was simple, comprehensible, striking, a clear testimony of the power of Jesus. The following Sunday a minister was preaching who came from the province of Brandenburg and was applying for a place in Berlin. He spoke about the same text. His sermon had the conventional structure and was peppered with little stories by way of explanation. We thought the difference must be obvious to everybody. But my father told us later that the Kirk Session had decided for the second preacher. The other they considered too refined, too highfalutin, too grand. They wanted something plain and simple. All attempts to persuade them were in vain: Bonhoeffer was rejected. Soon after that he went as a minister to London.

It is difficult to characterize the Bonhoeffer of those Berlin years. My memory has retained some moments of that time, whereas others have hardened into concepts, unconsciously. With astonishment I learned that he was a convinced socialist and a pacifist. This attitude was so incomprehensible that for a time I mistrusted his ethics. And simultaneously he gave us enthusiastic descriptions of Spain and praised the bull-fight as a great experience. He would not listen to any of our objections. That was permissible, he said, because genuine. Bonhoeffer had an aesthetic and a logical side to his mind; he also knew how to enjoy life. He was a planner on a grand scale, there was always a vital project to be pursued. In old papers I have noted down about him: 'Near and far away at the same time, keeping a distinguished distance and yet ready and open'. He has immense powers which are also immensely disciplined. Conflicts were experienced and borne by him in an almost 'holy' way. And he did have conflicts in his private life, just as we had.

# Seen with the Eyes of a Pupil

## FERENC LEHEL

I owe it to Karl Pröhle, my professor at the Hungarian Lutheran Theological faculty in Sopron (Oedenburg), that I came to Berlin and to Bonhoeffer. He procured me a travelling scholarship. First I went to Basel, where Professor Köberle, with his wide-ranging mind, held a colloquium on the problem of *Geist* in philosophy and theology. In the autumn of 1932 I proceeded to Berlin, where Eduard Spranger was lecturing on Kant's *Critique of Pure Reason*, and Nicolai Hartmann on the philosophy of Hegel.

In Berlin the licentiate Dietrich Bonhoeffer roused my interest. I went to see him. He was a strongly-built young man, twenty-six years of age, who looked more like a sportsman than a pastor or scholar. During the winter semester 1932–33 I enrolled for two of his lectures, 'Creation and Sin' and 'Recent Theology', and in the summer semester 1933 for a two-hour course on Christology and a two-hour seminar on Hegel's philosophy of religion.

He was an extremely inspiring personality and quite absorbed by the problems he was concerned with; therefore there was no room for sentimentality or rhetorical artifices. What attracted more and more students to the lectures of this young scholar was his Kierkegaardian depth, his Harnack-like ability for analysis, the profound way in which he saw things in their context, like Troeltsch, his knowledge of his material, in which he resembled Holl, and his Barth-like singleness of mind. We followed his words with such close attention that one could hear the flies humming. Sometimes, when we laid our pens down after a lecture, we were literally perspiring.

I was often his guest in the Bonhoeffer house, Wangenheim

Strasse 14. What the Bonhoeffer family offered for the enjoy-
ment of the mind as well as the body was on the same high level.
When we felt we should refuse an invitation to a meal, he
assured us: 'That is not just my bread, it is *our* bread, and when
it is jointly consumed there will still be twelve baskets left over.'
Such was his humour.

The interest, the concern with which he met me, convinced
me of his genuine ecumenicity. In everyday matters he was
helpful too. He gave me directions for the loveliest excursion
of my life, which I made with my friend, who later became
Bonhoeffer's successor as chaplain at the Technical College.
I rode Bonhoeffer's balloon-tyred bicycle. When I saw the
chalk cliffs of Sassnitz on the island of Rügen, I remembered
what he had often told us of the grandeur and overpowering
impression of God's creation. And before the war memorial of
Warnemünde his words about the discord and the destructive
power of sin came to my mind. There I understood his great
respect for Gandhi.

In my intellectual difficulties he stood by me, as a pastor,
brotherly and friendly. When he recommended Karl Heim's
*Glaube und Denken* to me he pointed out how Heim was able to
feel at one with the doubter; how he did not indulge in cheap
apologetics which from their lofty base fire upon the battlements
of natural science. We must think with the doubter, he said,
even doubt with him. This must have been something of a
confession of Bonhoeffer's. Such words can only be spoken by
a man who has grasped something of the mystery of the In-
carnation and for that reason cannot speak of it in doctrines.
He thought that Heim's alternative, belief or despair, was wrong,
as these two did not belong to the same dimension; here Bonhoeffer's later knowledge was already indicated which he
expressed in his unwillingness to make use of border situations.

When we talked about Bavinck's book, *Natural Science on its
Way to Religion*, he wondered whether in applying Planck's
quantum theory one was allowed to speak in such self-confident

tones of the dissolution of the causal-mechanical world view, and whether the construction of such a view was a necessary preliminary for the proclamation of the Church. The traffic on Jacob's ladder had not been a traffic from below to above. Thus Bonhoeffer proved that he was a good dialectical theologian. In these deliberations the distinction between faith and religion was already outlined. And there is more behind them, what Bonhoeffer has called a 'Resurrection-life'. Indeed, in the world come of age too – to use the later Bonhoeffer's words – there will be a Church, though in a different form. But the lord of the Church who can raise children to himself out of stones will give her a future if she throws herself into his arms.

# Drawn Towards Suffering
## GERHARD JACOBI

Dietrich Bonhoeffer was a person who reflected on and struggled with the most divergent thoughts, thoughts which often surprised his friends. It was not only theological or church questions that haunted him, but people troubled him too. With close interest he watched them drawing to one another and then again repulsing each other, and asked himself how this could be and found no answer. And there was also the world before his keen eyes, with its economic, social and cultural phenomena. How true community might come about between individual men or groups of men was a question he never solved.

Sometimes thoughts occurred to him which after a time surprised himself, and which he was able to drop again. When we went home together after the 'Brown Synod' he had the impulsive idea that the pastors who were opposed to the German Christians might be well advised to join the Lutheran Free Church. We went straight away to the pastor of the Lutheran Free Church in the Nassauische Strasse. There we learned that the pastors of the territorial church would be accepted if they brought with them five hundred members of their congregations. After only a few days Bonhoeffer dropped this plan.

He made a calm and harmonious impression upon the outside world. At meetings of pastors he spoke only briefly. Twice he quoted to them nothing but the words:

*One man asks: What is to come?*
*The other: What is right?*
*And that is the difference*
*Between the free man and the slave.*

He said nothing more, but those few words spoken in calmness and certainty, and out of personal freedom, found their mark.

In private conversation he made a less calm and harmonious impression. One noticed at once what a sensitive person he was, what a turmoil he was in, and how troubled. During such conversations he would express opinions which were both interesting and odd, then abandon them when it could be proved from biblical passages that the New Testament as a whole followed a different line of thought on this particular question.

If one may judge from what students of the Preachers' Seminary have said of the time when Bonhoeffer was its head, he must have been the calm and superior leader for them (which is of course necessary in such a living community), issuing clear and definite directions for the lives of the future pastors. But once in my study he confessed how many problems he had to face in this work too. At one time they were so overpowering that he seriously doubted whether this was the proper place for him. But I suppose that his students noticed nothing of all that.

Some of his spontaneous definitions he wrote down. He would have declined to develop from them as it were a whole theology. Even though his thoughts were clearly and precisely defined, they often became questionable again to him, especially when expressed in print or writing. I remember in particular how deeply a letter of Karl Barth affected and upset him, in which Barth criticised 'the basic distinction between theological work and edifying contemplation' as practised in Bonhoeffer's Preachers' Seminary (letter of 24th October 1936 in *Gesammelte Schriften* II, 287–91). He was especially agitated by Karl Barth's remark that what disturbed him in the seminary was a 'smell, hard to define, of a monastic eros and pathos'. Or the following event comes to my mind: Dietrich Bonhoeffer had given me a copy of his *Cost of Discipleship* with a special dedication of gratitude. When I read it, I told him I wondered whether two of his exegeses corresponded to the general line of the New Testament. He nodded in earnest agreement, but then waved it aside with his hand. He had already passed beyond his exegesis and was intent on something else.

All the same, we should read his occasionally off-putting remarks with attention. They have sprung from an alert mind which probed the depths and brought forth ever fresh things.

Bonhoeffer never doubted the Trinity. He would certainly have fought the fashionable coquetting with unbelief. But he was haunted by the question about the will of God *hic et nunc*. Here he looked far afield: he was not just concerned with Germany and National Socialism, but with all nations of the world with their needs and bewilderments, but also with the new things that emerged from them.

In this way he came across Gandhi. And he wondered whether Gandhi with his teaching of passive resistance, and with his life which personified passive resistance, did not represent God's will for the nations.

Something else attracted him to Gandhi. Dietrich Bonhoeffer had always had a deep understanding for the great value of suffering. Even before 1933 he was concerned about the western world, where right is enforced by war. On the other side he saw India where the people followed Gandhi's commandment: 'Do not destroy any life; it is better to suffer than to live by force.' It was Bonhoeffer's high regard for suffering, I think, which drove him to Gandhi. Later, after his long imprisonment and violent death, it has sometimes seemed to me that his understanding of suffering may have been born of an unconscious premonition of his own suffering.

In 1934 he wrote to his grandmother: 'I may go to the university of Rabindranath Tagore. Though I'd much rather go straight to Gandhi for whom I have very good recommendations from his best friends. I might spend six months there, or longer, as a guest. . . . At any rate it sometimes seems to me that "paganism" contains more Christian elements than our whole *Reich* Church. Indeed Christianity does come from the orient, and we have westernized it so much that we have lost it to the extent that we are now experiencing.'

In the years 1933 and 1934 I repeatedly warned him not to

go to India and told him plainly his place was in the German Church, especially during the 'Third Reich'. There was enough work to do there in witnessing to Jesus Christ as the Lord and in proclaiming the will of God. From London he often rang me up in the evenings, inquired about the Church struggle or reported how the Bishop of Chichester, George Bell (who in our telephone conversations figured under the pseudonym 'Uncle George'), estimated the present situation in the struggle between the Confessing Church and National Socialism. Once Dietrich Bonhoeffer rang me just to ask with a voice more restrained than usual, whether he might not be able to learn something from Gandhi, after all. I only answered: 'There is still enough for us to learn from the New Testament and the Reformers.' He agreed, thanked me and rang off. He only told me much later that, in November 1933, Karl Barth had given him the advice: '. . . you really ought to return to your post (in Berlin) by the next boat; or, shall we say, the next but one.'

At my instigation the Confessing Church called Bonhoeffer to a preachers' seminary which was to be set up. My main reasons were objective; but I also wanted to keep Bonhoeffer away from India by directing him towards a serious task to be done with young Germans. He was glad about this appointment and set about it with a certain passion. That a man who came from the most civilized background and was an eminent theological scholar should be so strongly drawn towards suffering, that he had to live through suffering and, to his last moment, suffered it in prayer, this is Dietrich Bonhoeffer's abiding greatness.

# III

---

1933    17th October, begins ministry in London

21st November, first visit to Chichester

1934    22nd–30th August, Ecumenical Youth Conference in Fanø

4th–8th September, with Jean Lasserre in Bruay

5th November, the London congregation breaks with the government of the *Reich* Church

25th November, to the Synod of the Confessing Church in Oeynhausen and Berlin, with Pastor Schönberger

1935    In January, to Berlin to discuss appointment at Seminary

15th April, farewell visit paid to Bishop Bell

# Some Weeks in London
## WOLF-DIETER ZIMMERMANN

For two reasons Bonhoeffer went to London in 1933 to serve a German-speaking congregation: first because he thought work in a parish important at this moment in history. He mistrusted the university. It was clear that the Church would have to find new ways to train her pastors. Nazism would not allow the theologians of the Confessing Church to do their work undisturbed much longer. Secondly, Bonhoeffer saw the need for ecumenical contacts, and for interpreting the situation of the German Church to foreign countries. He was not sure whether the churches of the *oikumene* would appreciate and join in the way of the Confessing Church. Bonhoeffer came into close contact with the Bishop of Chichester, and their association lasted even through the time of active resistance to Hitler during the war.

On Christmas Day I came to London to spend a few weeks with Bonhoeffer. The parsonage was situated on a hill in a southern suburb, Forest Hill. It was rather large, uninviting and cold. Only gas fires installed in the fireplaces heated the rooms, and of course they could not be kept going all the time. Cold, damp air penetrated through the windows. Thus we mostly lived in one room, and our morning baths were often reduced to a minimum.

At that time Bonhoeffer had his old friend Franz Hildebrandt living with him. They had been fellow students of theology in Berlin; but as a non-Aryan, Hildebrandt's future was threatened, and he sought a refuge outside Germany. A housekeeper looked after us, on an hourly basis, but everything else had to be done by ourselves, including the fight against mice which had nested in the house. For some time we had nobody to help us at all as the housekeeper had all of a sudden gone mad and had to be taken to a home. Religious madness, as Bonhoeffer informed us laconically.

Bonhoeffer and Hildebrandt were in a state of permanent dispute. Hildebrandt, a 'pupil' of Brunstäd, was an idealist, Bonhoeffer was a dialectical theologian. This dispute, serious and humorous, aggressive and witty, accompanied all events and meetings of the day. It gave the impression that these two people had nothing in common, and yet they were united by a deep friendship.

Usually we had a sumptuous breakfast about 11 a.m. One of us had to fetch *The Times* from which we learned, during breakfast, of the latest developments in the German Church struggle. Then each of us went about his own task. At 2 p.m. we met again for a light snack. Then there were conversations, interspersed with music, for both played the piano to perfection, solo or together. In the afternoons we mostly separated again. Many evenings we spent together at home, only occasionally going to see a film or a play, or to other engagements. Such evenings at home were typical of our life in London: theological discussions, music, debates, story-telling, all following one another, passing into one another – till 2 or 3 a.m. Everything broke forth with an enormous vitality. Sermons were made that way too: jotted down in the middle of a conversation, interrupted again by piano-playing. Hildebrandt thought Bonhoeffer was going the wrong way, and Bonhoeffer defended himself against Hildebrandt's 'positivism'. On many points there was no bridging the gap, there was just a never-ending dispute starting from different angles and always pointing to the same contrast of attitude. To the observer this seemed to be the beginning of a basic dissension and estrangement. But it all happened within a human relationship for which opinions did not mean anything ultimate. This mixture of meditation, discussion and music ('This is perfect, this is clear, there are no misunderstandings in this') has remained in my memory as typical of those weeks in London.

# Bonhoeffer without his Cassock
## LAWRENCE B. WHITBURN

My wife and I had the very great fortune of not only knowing Dietrich Bonhoeffer in church, but also in his private life. After Sunday service he would often walk home with us and 'just pop in for a moment' to have a chat about the sermon, the congregation or any other subject that came to mind. From this beginning there soon developed an unaffected friendship and it did not take very long before he was coming and going as freely as one of the family. A sign of this unaffectedness was the manner in which he unceremoniously brought along with him any visitors or immigrants who happened to be with him at the time – his friends were our friends, that was understood. In this way we also had the pleasure of meeting many interesting people, including Hildebrandt, Winterhager, Dr. Jehle, among others.

One particular Christmas Day remains unforgettable. We had invited Bonhoeffer to have Christmas dinner with us and as usual he brought one of his friends with him. We had obtained an enormous turkey, but when it appeared steaming on the table, the horrible fact emerged that none of us really knew how to carve a turkey correctly. I ought to have known this as an Englishman, but I had been many years abroad and in any case, the carving of poultry never was and still is not one of my strong points. Bonhoeffer did not hesitate very long, he would do it. Whilst we all held the unfortunate bird down, otherwise it would have landed on the carpet, Bonhoeffer went into the attack with the carving knife. We all fed fully and richly, but my wife and I will never forget the sight of that dissected skeleton. As we often remarked later – Bonhoeffer was capable of anything.

# I Knew Dietrich Bonhoeffer

Conversation covered all the subjects one can imagine. If one really wanted to raise a lively discussion, one had only to touch on the subject of divorce or pacifism. His opinion against the former and in favour of the latter was so marked and clear in his mind that the discussion soon developed into an argument, presumably as we thought the opposite. Nevertheless we still remained good friends.

Apart from the church and theology he had a second great interest – music. He played the piano very well and as I am also a singer, one of his favourite pastimes was to accompany me, as long as the accompaniment was really difficult or almost unplayable. He found particular pleasure in Loewe's ballads, among them especially 'Odin's Ride'. It did not seem to matter much that these ballads are extremely exhausting for the singer. I always had the feeling that he was seeking therein some form of relaxation, using the fullness and richness of the music as a form of 'work-out'. Bad music was for him unbearable and thereby hangs a tale. As is often the case, our congregation at that time had the bad habit of gradually getting slower during the hymns, a fault which unfortunately was also shared by the organist. Bonhoeffer decided that the correct tempo when singing hymns must be maintained and asked me to help. So, the following Sunday we went into battle, with the result that during the first hymn, we were soon a whole verse in advance. It was useless, we had to give up the fight. Thereupon Bonhoeffer thought we ought to form a church choir – I should conduct and he would sing with us. It would not be quite truthful to say that the practices always ran smoothly. Notwithstanding, to his great joy, we progressed well enough to sing carols under the Christmas tree the following Christmas.

One day his friend, Dr. Jehle, called to see him when he was out and decided therefore to await Bonhoeffer's return. In order to surprise him, he got the idea of hiding under the grand-piano and promptly fell fast asleep. Bonhoeffer came home and went straight to bed. During the night he was awakened by a strange noise and after some investigation, discovered Jehle snoring away under the piano. Like two small boys, the theologian and the scientist were highly delighted at this adventure. There was always an abundance of humour when Bonhoeffer was around. On another occasion he was playing a piano duet with my wife, one of Beethoven's pieces. The first chord, however, sounded like an excruciating dissonance. Just for fun Bonhoeffer had started in an entirely different key. He was fond of playing tennis, firstly to get his weight down, a matter that rather worried him, and secondly to get some exercise in the open air. If he lost, much to his disappointment, he would say, 'It's only lack of practice, you know.'

These are only small and unimportant details from Bonhoeffer's life, but they do show the versatility of this most prominent theologian and Christian. Unfortunately we were obliged to move to North London for business reasons, right on the opposite boundary of the capital and were then no longer able to participate in his church and private life. Nevertheless, Bonhoeffer often visited us in our new home – the long and tiresome journey from one side to the other did not count – he never forgot or neglected his former friends.

# Arresting the Wheel

## OTTO DUDZUS

The following scene is now widely known: During one of their daily walks round the prison yard in Tegel Dietrich Bonhoeffer was asked by a fellow-prisoner how as a Christian and a theologian he could take it upon himself to participate in the active resistance against Hitler. In the brief time given him under the eyes of the warders, he answered with a story: If he, as a pastor, saw a drunken driver racing at high speed down the Kurfürstendamm, he did not consider it his only or his main duty to bury the victims of the madman, or to comfort his relatives; it was more important to wrench the wheel out of the hands of the drunkard.

It was not only by taking part in the resistance movement that Bonhoeffer tried to arrest the wheel. It became his fate to work in opposition. Not because he inclined to this attitude, for by nature and upbringing he said yes rather than no. He was a man who would rather have helped to build a whole and sound order of things than to remove a perverted, destroyed order. Small events illustrate this more clearly than long reflections. On our return journey from the ecumenical conference in Fanø we had to change trains at the Danish frontier station, Süderlügum. The train to Hamburg was waiting on the opposite platform. We students took the easy way and just crossed over the rails. Bonhoeffer was the only one who took the rather long and tedious way down to and across the wooden bridge which spanned the rails. He made us feel that he had no patience for our disregard of a meaningful order. The smallest offence against order shocked him. For the sake of the order which had been destroyed on a grand scale, he became a revolutionary.

## Arresting the Wheel

I have rarely seen Bonhoeffer as a mere spectator of events, even where he could not have a direct influence, by his position or office. In this, his first-hand information about events in the State and Church proved useful to him, and also his gift of grasping a situation with extraordinary quickness. I vividly remember his activity during the Church elections of the summer 1933, whose consequence was that the German Christians seized power in the Church. I do not know what happened in the committees and behind the scenes, and how much part Bonhoeffer had in the deliberations and decisions. I only got to know him about that time. But what we heard by way of short reports before and after the intimations, made it certainly plain that here a man of intelligence and incorruptible clarity of vision resisted a fatal development and was not ready to accept what was born of stupidity, lies and brute force. Negotiations, discussions, standpoints and sermons all formed a unity. On such occasions Bonhoeffer's sermon was the last link in a long chain of activity, which surpassed all the rest by the way it was thought out to the last, brilliantly formulated and often strikingly effective. Bonhoeffer's final action during the Church elections was his sermon on election Sunday in Trinity Church in Berlin, on the text Matthew xvi, 13–18. He invited his listeners to search afresh for the destroyed, defiled, dishonoured Church in the biblical Word. In the midst of the multifarious 'opinions' around us, he said, truth is shining forth in the proclamation of the Word. Where people are about to destroy the foundations, the one true foundation comes to light and claims the whole man.

Without any doubt Bonhoeffer's intervention in ecumenical affairs had far-reaching consequences. From the autumn of 1933 he was the pastor of a German-speaking congregation in London. Karl Barth in his charming and humorous way had scolded him when he went there. He said that Bonhoeffer with his theological intelligence and his Germanic hero's figure belonged to the front line of the Church dispute; his departure from Germany was a flight; he had to return by the next ship, at the latest the next but one. Well, Bonhoeffer was never behind the front line.

Subsequently the work done in London proved to be a vital phase in the great dispute, and nobody but Bonhoeffer could have achieved this. For many years he had been secretary of the Youth Commission in the World Alliance for Promoting International Friendship through the churches, and as such had good contacts with the leaders of the Ecumenical Movement. These contacts were now made use of and developed in order to supply appropriate information about the events in Germany and to help the top committees of the Ecumenical Movement to judge and act steadily in the interest of the Church. He knew how to convince them that this was not an internal German affair, but that at this point the entire Church was challenged – that is, if the Church introduced the Aryan clause, and a 'leadership principle' with terrorist methods. Even then, Bonhoeffer was distressed by the vision of National Socialism forcing its methods and aims upon other countries and churches, and he expressed this fear often enough. His influence was considerable. He saw to it that the attempts of the *Reich* Church government to appease and deceive were hardly accepted anywhere in the Ecumenical Movement, least of all by the Bishop of Chichester. It must be mainly attributed to Bonhoeffer's actions that Chichester as President of 'Life and Work' decided to intervene with the authorities of the *Reich* Church, expressing in very polite terms, but none the less clearly, the deep alarm of the churches of the World Council about the Aryan clause and the leadership principle in the German Protestant Church (the so-called 'Ascension Message'). It was not in Bonhoeffer's nature to press people for a decision. In personal matters, it was my experience that he was always careful and reserved towards others. But there is no doubt that where the fate of the Church and Christianity in Europe were concerned, he was most audacious in urging the Bishop of Chichester to take a decision. His recurrent argument was that the hard-pressed congregations and pastors in Germany were waiting for such a word, that they must not be disappointed in their trust in the Ecumenical Movement, and that if they were this would have devastating effects on their relation to the other churches. With these arguments, Bonhoeffer probably went beyond the facts, for some of those hard-pressed German congregations were rather apprehensive about intervention by the Ecumenical Movement which might only make matters worse.

And now came the ecumenical conference in Fanø in Denmark, which had been awaited by the Protestant Christians of the whole world with intense eagerness. Its theme was to be: 'The Church and the Peoples of the World.' This was in the air. A new relation had to be found for the new phenomenon of States with a totalitarian *Weltanschauung*. The part Bonhoeffer played in the theme and in the course the conference took cannot be overestimated. He saw to it that it did not become a non-committal academic debate. The invitation from Geneva, asking Bonhoeffer to write a theological *exposé* for the main theme of the conference, said the question had to be put how the current problems might be tackled in the next two or three years. Bonhoeffer, however, saw these problems as so urgent that he did not even see fit to wait for two or three months.

But first an important preliminary question had to be solved. A few weeks before the conference began, Bonhoeffer suddenly cried off. The reason was that Geneva had invited a delegation from the *Reich* Church led by Bishop Heckel, but had taken no notice of the Confessing Church, which a few months earlier had been constituted at the Synod of Barmen and claimed to be the legitimate Protestant Church in Germany. (Bonhoeffer himself had not been invited as representative of the Confessing Church, but as secretary of the World Alliance.) Bonhoeffer pressed for an invitation to the Confessing Church but met at first with no encouragement. He was told that only representatives of churches which belonged to the Ecumenical Council were invited; that the Confessing Church had not applied for admission; if they hurried up and did so, they could be invited too. According to the regulations and usage of the Ecumenical Council this answer was correct and logical. But for the Confessing Church such an application would have meant self-surrender, for the whole world would have been given to understand that it saw itself as a second Protestant Church alongside the *Reich* Church. Again Bonhoeffer found an understanding advocate in the Bishop of Chichester. An invitation was sent to Präses Koch, the leader of the Confessing Church, and to a further representative chosen by the *Reich* Brethren's Council. In the discussion with the Geneva office about the problem of the invitation several arguments were in conflict with one another. Bonhoeffer already saw in the Ecumenical Movement what he wanted it to be, no longer a pragmatic association acting on legalistic and statistical principles, but a committee understanding itself as the Church and making decisions in the spirit and the interest of the Church. Bonhoeffer greatly regretted that the invitation was gratefully received but not accepted; but to take part officially at the meeting, in a time of high political tension, might have put an undue strain on the whole work of the Confessing Church. But for Bonhoeffer the way to Fanø was now open.

With the message of the Bishop of Chichester about the situation of the Protestant Church in Germany an important preliminary decision had been made. From the very beginning the president had planned to put the points of the message up for debate at the conference, and to make the Ecumenical Council decide whether they were to adopt the whole of the message, in its particular points. Bonhoeffer did not take part in the decisive meeting. He could now calmly await the course things would take. The official delegation of the *Reich* Church was certainly not in an enviable position. Who was to accept the assurance of the leader of the delegation that 'in the German *Reich* the free proclamation of the Gospel in word and print' was in no wise endangered, and that 'the general circumstances in present-day Germany even give far more possibilities to the proclamation of the Gospel than before'? The German speaker protested against interference with domestic German affairs, he called the president's message a transgression and protested against a German 'group' (the Confessing Church) being specially named in a partial and positive way. Nobody had the impression that this was a free vote of a church; the direct political orders from Berlin were easily recognizable, and as such embarrassing. Before the conference in Fanø began, the German Minister of the Interior had issued a warning against discussing the situation of the Church, and had threatened all those who informed foreign countries about church affairs with a trial for high treason. Members of the meeting reported later that the only point of the immensely long but not immensely clear speech of the leader of the German delegation must have been to fill all the available time and thus to prevent a discussion of the message, and the acceptance of a resolution. The Ecumenical Council, however, supported the message of its president. To stress its attitude, it elected two members of the Confessing Church to be its consultants, Präses Koch and Dietrich Bonhoeffer.

This meeting was an immense step forward on the way of the Ecumenical Movement from being a mere pragmatic association to becoming a church which understands itself as such and acts accordingly. I wonder if Visser't Hooft thought of this when once he said: 'Dietrich Bonhoeffer threw heavy lumps at our feet and said: "Pick them up"'? Anyway, this is a classic example of Bonhoeffer's superior insight. Diverse motives and thoughts found their precise expression in the same event. On the one hand Bonhoeffer was concerned to find help for the Confessing Church with this decision; in the midst of its dangers and tribulations in Germany, he wanted it to find support in the Ecumenical Movement. In his opinion such help implied that the Christians in Germany might learn to find

Christians as partners in dialogue within the Ecumenical Movement, and not Frenchmen, Englishmen, Americans and others in Christian camouflage; they might learn to leave their misconceived patriotism at home and to talk with the others in Christian openness. But Bonhoeffer was equally concerned about the Ecumenical Movement. In the preceding years of his work within the World Alliance, his one and only aim had been that this group of people might think and act purely from the basis and in the interest of theology and the Church. He saw the great chance for this, and helped to bring it about. Whenever, out of the very spirit of the Church, a decision was taken concerning the proclamation, teaching and order of the Church, as well as its relation to the world around it, such a decision was bound to have the most far-reaching consequences for the self-understanding of the Ecumenical Movement. It was hardly imaginable that it could ever retrace its steps from there. Bonhoeffer did not allow the thought to arise that this view was an interference with the internal affairs of a country, and thus he helped the Ecumenical Movement for the first time thoroughly to unmask the treacherous alibi of nationalist wilfulness.

However, Bonhoeffer's most passionate concern lay in another field. Simultaneously with the Ecumenical Council, the World Alliance for Promoting International Friendship through the churches met at Fanø. As mentioned above, Bonhoeffer had been asked to work out preparatory theses for the discussion. The study department in Geneva which commissioned him probably thought in terms of a thoroughly academic and non-committal definition of the relation between ecumenicity and internationalism, of theoretical reflections about the right and the limits of the Church's collaboration in the solution of international problems. Bonhoeffer saw these problems as extremely pressing. Germany had left the League of Nations, had cancelled all international agreements as far as they provided for a limitation of armaments, and had started on a feverish rearmament with the clearly discernible aim of preparation for war. Hindenburg's recent death had left Hitler's power absolute, without any control. Could the collaboration of the Church in solving international problems consist in anything but the call for peace? Bonhoeffer knew that now was the time to say the one necessary thing and nothing else. Therefore in his memorandum he restricted himself to the question of war and peace, and, by contrasting it with secular pacifism he sought to establish the proper starting-point for a Christian obligation to peace. He got a bad mark from the leader of the commission of studies in Geneva, as a pupil does for a poor essay, or one which does not take in all possibilities, and, somewhat condescendingly, he was referred to the bulky and profound material which was already at hand and might have assisted him in grasping the theme better.

On 28th August Bonhoeffer had to lead the morning prayers which took place every day for the participants of the conference. Normally this was a framework into which they willingly fitted themselves, perhaps a little by way of routine; but this service of worship became possibly the decisive, certainly the most exciting moment of the conference. Bonhoeffer always said the most important and also the most concrete things in his services. He always regarded the sermon as the last word, after many other words had been spoken (which is probably the only view of a sermon which is to the point). His text was Psalm lxxxv, 8: 'I will hear what God the Lord will speak: For he will speak peace unto his people, and to his saints.' He spoke of the Lord and his commandment within the political possibilities; of peace, which is not a problem, but a reality given with the appearance of Christ; of the Ecumenical Church as the indestructible community; of the impossibility of bearing arms against him who has become our brother in Christ, and in whom Christ himself would be hit; of the only way in which there will be peace. He called upon the great Ecumenical Council as the supreme court which could speak the word about peace with such authority that no worldly power could pass it over. Tomorrow, he said, the trumpet of war may sound; but today the Council is assembled and can by their word take the weapons from the hands of all those who believe in Christ. What are we waiting for?

From the first moment the assembly was breathless with tension. Many may have felt that they would never forget what they had just heard. An English politician who was present is said to have been annoyed about the defective sense of reality in the theologians. Was he still of that opinion a few years later? Bonhoeffer had charged so far ahead that the conference could not follow him. Did that surprise anybody? But on the other hand: could anybody have a good conscience about it?

This passionate call to a world Church which feels itself responsible for peace was for Bonhoeffer not an isolated affair which was broken off because it obviously found no echo. He stuck to this responsibility throughout all the complications and confusions, including his personal 'change' from a pacifist to an active resistance fighter. Even the Bonhoeffer of the conspiracy who clearly saw how far he had removed himself from his direct charge within the Church, and who, at least sometimes, asked himself whether this did not make him unfit for the service of the proclamation, even he can only be grasped within this ecumenical responsibility for peace. But to go into this would exceed the limits of this essay.

A report on Bonhoeffer's activity in Fanø would be incomplete if it did not at least mention how, in spite of all other demands upon him, he had always time for his pupils and friends who met him there again, how he entered into discussions with them, played with them, bathed with them in the stormy North Sea and was always ready for fun. During the comfortable speech delivered by a very voluminous dignitary of the Eastern Church, he pushed a piece of paper towards us on which he had scribbled Christian Morgenstern's rhyme: 'A fat cross on a fat belly – Who would not feel the breath of the deity?' But, strictly speaking, I should not thus have told on him.

# The Acts of the Apostle –
# Dietrich Bonhoeffer

## HENRY SMITH LEIPER

Of the various meetings which I had with Dietrich Bonhoeffer over a period of years between 1934 and 1939 there were just two involved detailed conversations shared only by the two of us. But it happens that these conversations took place at dramatic and crucial times in his life. And I believe that they afforded significant insights as to his capacity for decisive actions in line with his deepest loyalties and without counting the possible cost to himself.

When he was studying at Union Theological Seminary – which was my own place of training for the ministry – I was with him, but only in a casual way as a special lecturer. It was shortly after this, however, that we were both taking part in a meeting of the Executive Committee of the Stockholm Movement (Universal Christian Council for Life and Work). The meeting was held on the little island of Fanø off the coast of Denmark opposite Esbjerg, and in addition to the routine business there was to be a special inquiry concerning the confrontation of Christianity and Hitlerism in Germany. Those in attendance included prominent leaders of the churches in many lands, and of course the new leaders of the Evangelical Churches under the then recently 'elected' *Reich* Bishop Müller who had been picked by Hitler to replace the man the churches had truly elected, Dr. von Bodelschwingh of Bielefeld.

It is important to mention the above since Müller's representative at our meeting was Bishop Heckel who was in charge of German overseas pastors and chaplains. Dietrich had been appointed under the former administration to its congregation in London, yet by the time we got to Fanø his ecclesiastical superior was Heckel.

Knowing this, I was not surprised to have Dietrich come to my room, soon after the meetings had started, to talk about his problem. Nor was it surprising to have him say that Heckel had told him that he must leave London. This of course was an indication that Heckel knew what Dietrich felt about the attempts of Hitler and his German Christian followers to dominate the Church. When I asked what his reply had been to the Bishop's order, he said with a grim smile: 'Negative.' Amplifying that laconic remark he said: 'I told him he would have to come to London to get me if he wanted me out of that church.' With utter candour and fearless scorn he talked of what the followers of Christ must be prepared to do in resisting Nazi Caesarism and its penetration of spiritual domains. From this it was quite plain to me that he was prepared to fight the régime of Ludwig Müller. Yet at no point in our conversation did he show any concern for what might be the consequences of his decision to oppose openly the whole effort of Hitlerism to take over the control of the Church in Germany. Nor did he show the least doubt that the discerning Christians would have to deal realistically with the most dangerous and unscrupulous dictator who believed that he could achieve his plan for making what he called 'practical Christianity' a source of power and influence for his political platform.

It was very significant that Dietrich should have had such clear insights and could have reached such bold decisions so early in the official life of Hitler's thrust into the administrative life of the churches. From my own somewhat extensive experience in many earlier visits to Germany I knew that hardly any of his colleagues were as wise and fearless as he with respect to what was afoot. Nor were many of them as defiant – at least openly – towards the tyranny which had loomed on the horizons of their country in the 'miracle' of the Third Reich.

As will have been obvious from the events on the island of

Fanø, Dietrich was determined to approach the problems raised by the Nazi movement not merely from a theological or philosophical point of view but with directness of action.

These same characteristics came to expression in our next interview under quite different circumstances and in a wholly different setting. That interview is engraved on my memory, and it was, as then we could not have known, to be our last. It was about five years after the Fanø 'Life and Work' meeting and it took place at the National Arts Club in New York City. Dietrich had just arrived from Germany to undertake a sort of general chaplaincy in New York for the increasingly numerous refugees. He was invited by a combination of committees including the American Christian Committee for Refugees of which I was a founder and officer along with Reinhold Niebuhr, Paul Tillich and other friends of Dietrich. And our lunch together was for the purpose of discussing plans for Dietrich's new work. Those responsible for suggesting it quite definitely felt that there was a growing need for spiritual counsel such as a man like Dietrich could give with utmost effectiveness. Yet there was also the frank hope that we could save him from the growing hostility of the Hitlerites who feared and hated him. They were smarting under the humiliation of discovering that he had been able to carry on illegal theological education for many months despite all their vigilance.

What was my surprise and dismay to learn from my guest that he had just received an urgent appeal from his colleagues in Germany to return at once for important tasks which they felt he alone could perform in the resistance movement he had already served so effectively. I did not press him for details of what that work might be. Yet it was abundantly clear from his manner and his tenseness that he felt it something he could not refuse to undertake. It was soon clear to me that he had already determined his course of action – and it was *action* just as it had been five years earlier when he discussed with me another demand for his return to Germany! Nothing he said to me this time indicated whether he had any foreboding that what was ahead might involve grave consequences for him as a person.

Here again the stress was on action. Nothing was said about the theological basis on which his decision was made. But, knowing him, I had no doubt that there were profound impulsions motivating him as he 'set his face steadfastly towards (not) Jerusalem', but Berlin. Our parting was outwardly matter-of-fact; but I saw him leave with mixed feelings. Dominating my emotions was admiration such as I had felt at Fanø when he announced his defiance of Bishop Heckel. Clearly he felt this new summons to return was a call of God as that earlier one had not been. To the call of God he could give only one answer. But yet there was also in my mind a fear that grave consequences for my friend might flow from this decision. How grave those consequences were to be we now know only too well!

Needless to say, I never saw him again. Often as I pass the table in the National Arts Club where we lunched together that day I relive the hour of Dietrich's momentous decision for bold action. He was surely a good soldier of the Captain of our Salvation who had, long centuries ago, taken the road to Golgotha as he 'set his face steadfastly towards Jerusalem.'

# Contacts with London
## JULIUS RIEGER

In 1933 the pastor who looked after the German Reformed St. Paul's Church and the German Evangelical Congregation of Sydenham, in London, wanted to retire. He suggested that I should take over these two congregations in addition to my own, and employ a permanent colleague to help me out. Nothing came of this plan. So the Foreign Office of the German Evangelical Church was approached and soon a pastor was found who was willing to come to London. It was Dietrich Bonhoeffer.

Just then I had some business in Berlin and took the opportunity to meet my future London colleague. I received the impression of a kindly and extraordinarily intelligent man with whom one could at once feel at ease. Yet he did not wear his heart on his sleeve and obviously knew more than he said. He said nothing of his studies and his extensive experience of foreign countries, and I learnt only later of the time he had worked as a curate in Barcelona, and of his year at Union Seminary in New York – in fact his English had a pronounced American accent. We talked of our work in London and the problems of congregational co-operation which we practised there.

Bonhoeffer stayed in London for a year and a half. It was the only time in his life when he was fully employed and active as a parish minister. In this time he got to know the never-ending detail in the life of a congregation of the *diaspora* in a foreign country. In May 1934 he wrote home: 'It is really incomprehensible that so much should happen in so small a congregation.' Moreover he did not find it easy to preach twice on a Sunday.

Bonhoeffer seldom talked about himself. He was not the type to put all his wares in the shop-window. Only very rarely did he open up, and then it was like a dark landscape being lit up for a moment. This happened, for instance, when he once mentioned casually that in a certain church in Rome, I forget which, he had felt sorely tempted to become a Roman Catholic. Or when he mentioned, incidentally and quite freely, how ghastly it must be to reach the age of forty – he would never live to see that. In fact his life ended nine weeks after his thirty-ninth birthday.

During theological discussions he often expressed himself in ways that stuck in one's mind. 'From a dogmatic point of view, Harnack was a heretical teacher.' 'If something is said in the Bible it must have a meaning.' Once we were told that some Roman Catholic congregations prayed for the imprisoned and persecuted members of the Confessing Church; when some of us did not see anything remarkable in this, Bonhoeffer reacted sharply, saying: 'I am not indifferent to somebody praying for me.'

In a discussion somebody expressed the opinion that pacifism was really shirking one's duties. Bonhoeffer replied that it required more courage to be a pacifist and bear the consequences of this attitude than to submit passively to military service.

For a long time Bonhoeffer had wished to go to India and find out for himself what it was like. He felt drawn towards the country where the art of inwardness and meditation, of silence and concentration had not been forgotten, and the longer this fascination lasted for him the stronger it became. He was drawn as though magnetically by a man like Gandhi, who thought more highly of the Sermon on the Mount than most Christians do and who, by means of passive resistance, had achieved his political aims against a first-class world power.

From England the long-cherished plans of a journey to India could be more easily put into practice; Bishop Bell wrote to Mahatma Gandhi who immediately sent an invitation. Gandhi's invitation was for two people: Bonhoeffer was allowed to bring a friend. As a consequence he confided in me, and together we made serious plans for this voyage to India. Our prepara-

tions, however, came to an untimely end. For it was obvious
that the theological candidates of the Confessing Church had
to be trained in seminaries – a pressing need which could no
longer be postponed – and so Bonhoeffer's speedy return to
Germany was required of him.

Before that, however, we did have a journey together, not to
India but to the Midlands. At the end of March in 1935 we
visited some Anglican monasteries, and I shall never forget
those few days. The most important places of that kind are the
'Society of the Sacred Mission' in Kelham (founded in 1893),
the 'Community of the Resurrection' in Mirfield (founded in
1892), and the 'Society of St. John the Evangelist' in Oxford
(founded in 1865 by R. M. Benson), whose members are
commonly called 'The Cowley Fathers'.

Those three organizations have one thing in common,
namely, their remarkable achievement in the training of young
Anglican priests. On the other hand each individual community
has its own tradition. The difference of atmosphere in the three
houses has been characterized by the witty but pertinent remark
that in Oxford, tobacco is anathema and smoking strictly
prohibited, in Mirfield you may smoke, in Kelham you have to.

And indeed in Kelham we were received by a bearded lay-
brother whose pipe never seemed to go out. The venerable and
gifted founder of Kelham, old Father Kelly – sometimes described by the English as a theological precursor of Karl Barth
– was a chain-smoker. We smiled when we saw that the front
of his monk's habit was covered with cigarette ash. He brought
into his lecture-room a medium-sized pail containing an in-
flammable chemical, and now and then he dipped a wooden
stick into it when the cigarette in his long holder had burnt out
and a new one had to be lit. A number of his brilliant lectures
were for sale in mimeograph, and we certainly did not miss this
chance. Many months later Bonhoeffer asked me to send on to
him in Germany some of the copies which he had left behind in
London.

This 'tour of the monasteries' left us with many new impressions but also with all sorts of questions. There was the regular hourly prayer, which seemed like a strait-jacket and yet formed the students and made possible a Christian community outside the Roman Church which was realized several times a day. I think it was Father Kelly who replied to our question: 'How do you keep it up?' in the paradoxical words: 'I can do it, because I cannot.' Then, there was the problem of 'the devotional life', that concept which has flourished in the soil of the Church in the English-speaking world for which there has never been an adequate translation in German. There was the problem of teaching our own theological students that scholarly work on the Scriptures was not enough, but had to be accompanied by meditation on biblical passages. There was the freedom in their community life, which we could not help noticing during our visits – the Anglican monks played tennis or football in their free time. There was the secret strength of silence which the Protestant, with his love of disputation, is inclined to depreciate. And lastly, there was the difficult problem: guests from one of the Free Churches, or one of the Protestant Churches of Europe, were not allowed to participate in the sacrament of Holy Communion.

A few weeks after our journey, Bonhoeffer became the principal of the Preachers' Seminary of the Confessing Church, first in Zingst and then in Finkenwalde. Others have told how he put into practice the impulses he received in England. Bonhoeffer did not lose contact with us in London. He must have been in England at least four times in 1935 (in April, May/June, August, October). The relationship with England and with where he had worked previously proved to be stronger than he himself had first thought.

In Berlin we met whenever I was there (July and October). Each time we exchanged news which could not be entrusted to the post. In 1936 we met only once, as far as I remember, on 26th July in Berlin-Dahlem. But we had two 'middlemen' who kept us in close touch with one another. One of them was Pastor Franz Hildebrandt, who became my friend. As Niemöller's assistant and an intimate friend of Bonhoeffer he was assiduous in maintaining contact with London; and when I was in Berlin we met as often as possible. The other middleman was Wolfgang Büsing, a student at Finkenwalde, who joined us in London in 1936 for nine months as a curate; in the congregation of St. George's he was of great help in looking after the immigrants and refugees.

In the middle of February 1937 we welcomed Bonhoeffer back in London once again. He had come for a meeting of the Ecumenical Youth Commission. He gave an extensive account of recent events in the Church in Germany at our pastors' conference in which, among others, Dr. Hans Böhm from Berlin took part, and Dr. Otto Piper who had emigrated from Germany. On the following Sunday, the 21st February, his old congregation of St. Paul arranged an evening for all members to meet him.

I returned his visit in Berlin during the stirring weeks of June. There was some excitement about the question who should be sent to the Ecumenical Conference which was to meet in Oxford in July. Twice a session of the Prussian Brethren's Council in which I took part had to be broken off and removed to another place because the Gestapo were on our track. On the same evening, the 17th June, four meetings of the Confessing Church took place in the largest churches of Berlin; Niemöller had to give two successive addresses in the church of the Hohenzollern Platz because it could not hold the crowds. Later we met in Café Hohnen at the Nollendorf Platz; young Gollwitzer stood in the front garden directing us across the dance-floor to a secret back-room where the collections were counted and where Asmussen made one of his most moving speeches. Over and above all this a wave of arrests had begun whose end could not be foreseen: Freudenberg, Jacobi, Niesel were arrested while I was in Berlin, and we expected the same fate for Niemöller, which in fact happened on 1st July. My friends feared that the frontiers might be closed, and this made it advisable for me to abandon my railway ticket and fly back to London, which I did. In this uncanny atmosphere I met Dietrich Bonhoeffer and Franz Hildebrandt, the first time in the Stadtkrug Restaurant at the Zoo, the second time at the Stettiner Station. And I also experienced, besides all this, the soothing peace of a normal middle-class German family in Dietrich's home in the Marienburger Allee 43.

In the middle of March 1939 he was back in London, but not alone: he brought a young friend of his whom we had not met before, Eberhard Bethge. Both spent five weeks in England, and a list of their activities at that time might suggest that it was a happy and carefree holiday.

But the appearances were deceptive. When on 3rd April we returned to London, after a meeting in St. Leonard's, Bonhoeffer interrupted his journey in Bexhill, where Professor Reinhold Niebuhr from New York was making a short stay. We learnt only later that Bonhoeffer told him of the probability that war would break out in the autumn, and of his wish to receive an invitation to the United States for the summer.

The other problem which stirred him deeply and played a central part in our conversations of that time was what he should do if he was conscripted by the German Army. Two conversations which he had in those days were decisive for him. One was with the Bishop of Chichester. Dr. Bell, who had no children, spoke with him like a father to his son, as Bonhoeffer himself afterwards said. Dietrich as well as the Bishop spoke of their exchange of thoughts at that meeting as touching the very roots of Christian existence.

The other conversation was with Visser't Hooft and took place on the platform of Paddington Station in London. It was the first time that Bonhoeffer met him, and it was the same question which was discussed at this utterly prosaic place in the British capital.

Bonhoeffer later gave an account of both conversations. I had the impression that he had long before decided to be a conscientious objector, and that all he wanted was a brotherly and ecumenical confirmation of this decision. It would not have been enough for him to have the approval of people from a strictly pacifist camp. We must not forget that neither Bell nor Visser't Hooft was ever a pacifist. On 18th April we went to Germany together. It was a memorable journey. We crossed the channel in a gale. At Aachen we passed the German frontier and when I, as a German living in a foreign country, expressed my joy, regardless of all political problems and tensions, to be back in the home country, which was still beautiful, Bonhoeffer replied: 'We are entering a beautiful prison.'

In the next few weeks his plans for the United States became more definite and at the beginning of June the time had come: he left by way of London. What happened after that is well known: in the middle of July Bonhoeffer was unexpectedly back with us in London. The reasons for his surprisingly quick return to Europe were not grasped by all his friends. One of his arguments was that to stay in the United States had become impossible for him, for the news about the Church's struggle for existence in Germany had been publicized by the Americans so heedlessly that it exposed the German opposition to the gravest dangers.

On 16th July Dietrich told us about his American experiences in his sister's house in Forest Hill; on the 20th he, Franz Hildebrandt and I met in St. George's in Alie Street, and on the 24th my diary bears the short note: 'Lunch (Chinese) with Dietrich, at Liberty's, and in the Central European Travel Agency, Church Street, Kensington.' There had been so many meetings in recent years that we had no premonition that this was to be our last in this life.

On 3rd September 1939, a Sunday morning, the British Prime Minister informed Parliament that Great Britain and Germany were at war. It was my conviction that in time of war a pastor had to stay with his congregation. But the more difficult question was what was to become of my family. German nationals were allowed to return to the home country in the first few days of the war, and we decided that my wife and children should make use of this opportunity. We wrote to our fatherly friend, the Bishop of Chichester, telling him of the imminent split-up of the family. He answered by return of post asking my wife to take with her three short letters with greetings for Pastor Dr. Böhm of the Provisional Government of the Confessing Church, for Frau Niemöller and for Dietrich Bonhoeffer.

Soon, however, we began to doubt whether our initial decision was the right one, and some days later we decided that the family should stay together in the new situation created by the outbreak of war. So the letters remained undelivered.

The letter of the Bishop of Chichester to Bonhoeffer ran as follows:

*My dear Dietrich,* 6th September 1939
You know how deeply I feel for you and yours in this melancholy time. May God comfort and guide you. I think often of our talk in the summer. May He keep you. Let us pray together often by reading the Beatitudes; *Pax Dei quae superat omnia nos custodiat.*

Your affectionate

*George*

In the first July days of 1942 a notable conference took place in the beautiful rooms of Newnham and Selwyn Colleges in Cambridge. The Bishop of Chichester had invited all German pastors who belonged to the 'Christian Fellowship in War Time', which he had founded in 1940.

It was the most natural thing in the world that at this Cambridge conference the Bishop of Chichester should tell us of his journey to Sweden, from which he had returned only a few weeks earlier. The great mutual trust which existed between the Bishop and his hearers was borne out by the fact that he told us all the details of his meeting with Schönfeld and Bonhoeffer in Stockholm and Sigtuna. Not one of those present at the Cambridge conference ever abused that confidence. On this occasion most of us heard for the first time of the plans of the German resistance movement, its readiness for action and especially of the personal involvement in it of Bonhoeffer whom we had hitherto known as a determined pacifist. In 1942 he was concerned, as we know, about the moral support which the Allies might give to the German resistance. It is idle to imagine what the world would look like today if Bonhoeffer's request in Sigtuna had met with more sympathy, understanding and support.

These were the last greetings of Dietrich Bonhoeffer which reached us, at that Cambridge conference in July 1942. On 5th April 1943 he was arrested in Berlin.

On 30th May 1945 I received a telegram from Geneva. It was in English and ran as follows: 'Just received sad news that Dietrich Bonhoeffer and his brother Klaus have been murdered in Concentration Camp Clossburg (*sic*) near Neustadt about 15 April short time before reached by American Army – stop – Please inform family Leibholz and his friends – stop – We are united in deep sorrow and fellowship – Freudenberg.' Dr. Freudenberg had been caught by the war in Switzerland, where he was holidaying in 1939, and has since then devoted himself to the important tasks of the refugee service in the ecumenical central office in Geneva.

I prefer not to speak about the emotions which this cable aroused in us. On 31st May I went to Oxford where the Leibholz family lived. I transmitted the news to his relatives and could not think of anything better than to read, in that troubled hour, Matthew x, the chapter that Dietrich had os impressively interpreted in his *Cost of Discipleship*.

The news was also flashed to Germany by the BBC, and thus the relations and friends in Berlin heard of the violent death of our brother for whom so many of us had feared and for whose safe keeping so many had prayed.

# IV

1935   26th April, beginning of the Preachers' Seminary at the Zingsthof (Baltic Sea)

24th June, st rt in Finkenwalde

6th September, application to the church government for erection of a Brethren House

1936   In February, last lecture within the Berlin Faculty on 'Discipleship'

29th February–10th March, study excursion of the Preachers' Seminary to Denmark and Sweden

5th August, deprived of right of lecturing at the University

13th November, Werner Koch arrested and later taken to a concentration camp

1937   11th September, end of semester in Finkenwalde, holidays in Bavaria

Middle of October, Preachers' Seminary closed down by the police

November, twenty-seven former students of Finkenwalde in prison

Publication of *The Cost of Discipleship*

5th December, beginning of team curacies in Köslin and Gross-Schlönwitz

# Finkenwalde

## WOLF-DIETER ZIMMERMANN

Finkenwalde is a tiny place, with a few houses, near Stettin. There the Confessing Church had started an illegal Preachers' Seminary. It looked primitive; the furniture consisted mainly of gifts from friends. Bonhoeffer had brought his books as there were hardly any theological works. The students worked in teams of three in rooms which were often just furnished with a desk, a shelf and some chairs. And yet many of them managed to make them look comfortable, by various means. The young theologians, about twenty-five in all, slept in one big room crowded with beds. For relaxation and diversion they had a large garden behind the house, walks alongside the near-by river, an occasional excursion to the sea.

A Brethren House was attached to the Preachers' Seminary. There some older seminarists lived who had stayed on and formed a close brotherhood. We envied them a little because each had his own room and wash-basin, and other privileges.

To arrive in these surroundings was a shock for us. Most of us came from 'solid' families, where everything was laid on. Now we were thrown into a makeshift existence where we found little of what we were accustomed to. When this external shock had been more or less overcome, we experienced the inner shock. We were pressed into a hard order of life. In the mornings, there was half an hour of silent meditation on one biblical text in Luther's translation; the same text for a week. We were not allowed to consult the original text, a dictionary or other books during this period. Two hours' rest after lunch. At night, to bed in silence. From the beginning we revolted against such a 'methodism'. There was too much 'must' for us. Bonhoeffer explained to us what help we should derive from this strict order. What we experienced, however, at least at the beginning, was emptiness in ourselves and in the texts, where knowledge and answers had been promised to us.

Each Saturday evening Bonhoeffer addressed us, as a pastor, guiding us to live in brotherhood, and working out what had been experienced during the last week, and what had gone wrong. Thus we gradually grasped that this experiment in life together was a serious matter. And gradually we became ready to fall in with him and to do with zest what we were asked to do. It did not come to very much, though. The time of meditation still did not grow into a time of revelation; the text did not speak to us, and if it did, it was in our own voice. We complained to Bonhoeffer about this failure, and it was decided to meditate together, and not in silence, once or twice a week. With the help of what others found in the text, we at least got an idea of what was meant by the word meditation. All of us had been too much bent on exegesis and application of the text. We had not known what it means that the word preaches itself. Only through long times of waiting and quiet did we learn that the text 'may be our master'. Half an hour of concentration: it is amazing what comes into your head during that time. The mind moves around, memories arise, dreams awaken. Sudden anger flares up. When we told Bonhoeffer of this, he said that was all right; things have to come into the open; but they must also be tamed in and through prayer. Everything that is suddenly there must be worked out in prayer. For many of us that half hour remained a burden to the end. But it taught all of us that the biblical word is more than a 'subject' which can be handled *ad libitum*. A text which had been meditated on can no longer be dissected into different sources and layers. The power of the word, just as it is transmitted, is only felt by him who bows before that word.

Bonhoeffer suggested that we hold a common hour of prayer early on Whitsunday. We assembled full of expectation, scepticism, curiosity. With a loud voice, he read to us the Whitsun text. After that, we sat together in silence. Here and there, somebody said a few words, another expressed his thoughts, a third prayed for something special. Nothing more happened. Bonhoeffer said a closing prayer which soberly and objectively directed us to the present time and barred all hopes for a new miracle. We had hoped this Whitsun would become a day of special inspiration, but it became a day of knowledge instead, calling us to faithful service in everyday matters and to obedient action without anxiety or *hybris*.

Soon after, on a Saturday evening, Bonhoeffer talked to us about confessing, brother to brother. There was to be a communion service the next day. In deep earnest, he spoke to us, stressing the urgency of it, but leaving us the freedom of personal decision. He said if we wished to be free we would have to make a clean breast of the grudges we bore one another. So, on this evening, we went to see one another and spoke of the many grievances stored up in the last few weeks. It was a great surprise to realize how we had hurt the other person, without intention, by chance, almost *en passant*. Now we knew what it meant to consider other people. The atmosphere was pure again, we could go to communion together without bearing a grudge against anyone among us. We were never given such a 'starting signal' again, but the beginning which was made was continued in many pastoral conversations. Sometimes it was a confession, sometimes a request for advice. At the end Bonhoeffer suggested we should each choose a brother who would accompany our life in intercession – as an outward sign, as it were, that even in the worst calamity we were not alone. My room-mate, Otto-Karl Lerche, asked me for this service. I was extremely surprised that anybody should expect it from me, and ask me spontaneously. For years after that we were in touch with one another, till he was reported as missing at the front.

The spiritual order was what was new to us, a burden difficult to bear, a discipline to which we did not like to submit. We made jokes about it, mocked at this cult and behaved like stubborn asses. Pietism and enthusiasm were for almost all of us a form of Christianity which we rejected. Prayers in the mornings and evenings, meditations, periods of silence – it was too much. We were not accustomed to keep quiet if we had words that could be spoken. Yet, apart from being a salutary exercise, this 'method' was a way of making the common life of so many people bearable. Bonhoeffer later told us that this second point of view had been very important for him.

Homiletics, catechetics, pastoralia, exegesis, all these were taught by Bonhoeffer alone, mostly with carefully prepared manuscripts. For sermon exercises we were mostly given difficult or very theoretical biblical texts whose 'course of action' we had to write down in the form of theses. The different drafts were read out. At the end he placed before us his counter-draft. Thus he persuaded us again and again that this particular text could be preached on – which, on the basis of our own attempts, we had doubted.

Our leisure time was catered for too, with music, table-tennis, bathing. Hardly any of us ever succeeded in beating Bonhoeffer at table-tennis. He was, officially, the principal of the Preachers' Seminary. But we were not allowed to address him like that. At that time the word 'brother' still had a good meaning for us, it was a sign of community, and we used it as such. Sometimes we enjoyed addressing Bonhoeffer as 'Mr. Principal' in public, say at a petrol station. He did not like it. He thought there should be one title only in the Church, that of pastor.

In the house we all had certain duties to fulfil, and to lend a hand in practical things. In the course of such duties, I happened to knock down an icon which belonged to Bonhoeffer. I somehow brushed against it, it fell from the wall and coloured bits crumbled off it. It looked terrible. I expected to hear hard words, for I knew how Bonhoeffer loved it. But nothing of the sort happened. He looked calmly at me and said : 'Such things

do happen; do not take it tragically; one must accept facts.'
One of the seminarists tried, in hours of finicky work, to glue
the little pieces on again, and he almost succeeded.

From Finkenwalde we went to Lower Pomerania on a
'Mission to the People'. This was to be the practical application
of what we had learned in theory. We had planned house
visitings, possibly ending with prayers, and addresses in the
church every evening. For this a text was chosen, say the
Prodigal Son, and divided into four parts each of which had to
be preached on, for five to eight minutes, by one of us. We spent
a long time thinking about what might be said in this situation,
and how it might be said. We prepared drafts, which were
mostly ruthlessly torn to shreds by Bonhoeffer and the others.
And gradually we learned to see the point, and how to speak
colourfully. In practice, this kind of evangelizing proved itself,
at least in the very traditional Lower Pomerania. At that time
Bonhoeffer also got into close contact with the Kleists in
Retzow and Schmenzin, a relationship which was to last all
his life; the 'Prussian' form of Christianity which they embodied
was deeply akin to his own.

# Dietrich Bonhoeffer in Pomerania

## WERNER KOCH

### *1. My Journey to Finkenwalde*

Sometimes, when I am out in my car, it happens that a man in a green uniform and white crash helmet stands in the middle of the road and lifts his sign, Stop: Car Control. 'Your driving licence, please.' And there he can read the official notice that I once dwelt in Finkenwalde, Pomerania, and that the office of the district of Randow had issued me a driving licence on 28th November 1935.

The writer of this article *also* took part in the seminary which the leaders of the Confessing Church had established in Finkenwalde for its future pastors. Though, if Dietrich Bonhoeffer had not been the head of this theological school, I should probably never have gone to Pomerania except for holidays. But in fact I stayed for almost six months. To be allowed to learn from Dietrich Bonhoeffer, to live with him under one roof, promised to be a very special experience. Even then, when his name had only just begun to shine. And especially then, at a time so full of decisions.

Unforgettable is that first journey to a place of such expectations. I boarded the express train to Stettin at the Stettiner Station, which at that time was known to every child in the capital of the *Reich*. The train was rather crowded, so I slowly squeezed myself and my suitcase along the narrow corridors of the long coaches in search of a seat. Before one compartment I stopped short, as if struck by a thunderbolt. I saw four young men in eager and happy conversation with another, still young-ish man whose high brow at once betrayed the scholar. Before I knew what I was doing I opened the sliding door and asked

Bonhoeffer at
Zingst in 1935

Taking a seminar in the dunes

courageously: 'Excuse me, are you gentlemen travelling to Finkenwalde?' I said Finkenwalde, though the train only went to Stettin where one had to change trains for Finkenwalde. The conversation stopped abruptly. Quick glances were exchanged. Bonhoeffer was the first to compose himself and answered: 'Yes indeed, we are going to Finkenwalde. Why does that interest you?' I said my name and was greeted with cheerful shouts. How on earth had I had the idea just to ask whether they went to Finkenwalde of all places? They did not think they looked so 'theological' but like 'quite normal people'. I simply said: 'I knew it somehow – that must be them, the brethren.' Another strange fact was that I had seen Dietrich Bonhoeffer the day before in two quite different parts of Berlin. I told him this, and he would not calm down about it: 'But you did not know me, or have you seen a picture of me?' I said no, but described to him in detail where I saw him, once in the street at the Zoo, and another time in a small café in Dahlem. A Roman Catholic Christian would perhaps say: 'I felt that I met a saint.' I should like to say today: I felt directly: that is he – a man signed by God, set apart for the coming martyrdom.

During our whole journey Dietrich Bonhoeffer kept returning to this strange event and it was one of the first things he told the seminarists from Pomerania who were already in Finkenwalde when we arrived.

Every detail of Finkenwalde remains clear in my memory: the former boys' school and its gymnasium which by the simplest means was changed into a church hall. The wonderful beech forest not far from the house, and some little lakes whose names I forget. And the road to Stettin which saw my first endeavours to gain the afore-mentioned driving licence – that road which one evening, at the beginning of December 1935, without any warning, acquired a spiderweb-thin layer of ice, so that I, with Bonhoeffer sleeping peacefully beside me, suddenly slithered into a merry-go-round and landed in a ditch. But the only result was that the members of the

Confessing Church in Stettin, who were waiting to hear an address from Bonhoeffer, had to go on heartily singing confessional hymns to fill in the time.

## 2. *Frau von Kleist-Retzow's town house in Stettin*

Stettin and the house in the Pölitzer Strasse 103 – who knows today what a centre of the spirit this was? In this house lived one of the most remarkable women of her time, Ruth von Kleist-Retzow. I had so far had little opportunity of meeting a representative of the great Pomeranian families personally. Now through Frau von Kleist, to whom Dietrich Bonhoeffer introduced me, I became aware of what Pomeranian aristocracy of the best kind meant: standing up to the last for truth and for right, and this permeated with so much goodness and wisdom, and everything rooted in and always nourished by Holy Scripture.

Of course such a woman at once saw through all the outward splendour of the Third Reich, perceived the decay at its roots and in deep alarm turned away from it. Her judgement was incorruptible, and she also wished that her grandchildren might clearly tell the difference between being and appearance. To this end she rented a spacious apartment in the Pölitzer Strasse of Stettin and gathered round her all those grandchildren of hers who attended the secondary schools in Stettin. She founded a sort of Kleistian family boarding-house where, in defiance of the *Zeitgeist,* the whole course of the day was to be determined by a Christian spirit and a Prussian sense of duty. What a contrast to the brown demon which filled the streets and squares of the town with its noise, with parades and fanfares, and with the sanguinary speeches of those who prepared the Germans for war – civilians and troops alike – under the slogan: Might before Right.

Now in this Kleistian family boarding-house everybody was woken early in the morning. The children had to get up at once, leave their beds and keep five minutes of silence for their morning prayers. As far as I remember, the old lady did not preside at the breakfast table, but with sovereign authority and inimitable warmth of heart she reigned over the big lunch-table, after her numerous and happy crowd had come home from the different schools of the town. One after the other they told her what had happened at school. If, which was not uncommon, a teacher had perverted the truth in favour of National Socialist ideology, she at once energetically put matters right.

In the afternoon Grandmother Kleist supervised the home-work; when the tasks seemed too difficult, she knew how to help out with her own rich knowledge and education. Dinner, at a fixed time, saw everybody round the table again. The conversa-tion was carried on in French, partly because this was Prussian tradition since the days of Frederick the Great, partly because it proved helpful for school. As my French was reasonably good, I was a welcome guest at these conversations.

Dinner was followed by prayers – not ready-made ones which were read out, but Grandmother Kleist herself expounded the texts on which she had reflected during the day. She had acquired such a knowledge of Scripture as I have rarely met. Scripture mentions 'prophetesses' as, for example, the pro-phetess Anna in the Christmas story of St. Luke, and I wonder if Grandmother Kleist was not such a person. Though she suffered under the falsehood and shame of that time as few Germans did, like Anna she never tired of 'giving thanks to God' and counting on his direct action and intervention.

Therefore she loved the Confessing Church, and was ever watchful of the dangers which might threaten it from within and without. Therefore, too, she was ready to take risks and to make sacrifices in order to carry on the work of the Con-fessing Church by external means as well. The Kleist lands and properties belonged to the Lord, and she acted accordingly. When the seminary's stores ran out (and the seminary had to train the 'servants of the Lord'), and, indeed, before such a thing happened, help from the Kleists was at hand: a cartful of potatoes, meat, vegetables, eggs, money. When a refuge was needed, it was found on one of the Kleist estates. For Bonhoeffer this family felt a deep veneration and friendship.

## 3. Letters from Stettin and Klein-Krössin

Before me I have letters written in the large, clear, almost masculine handwriting of the resolute old lady. It is twenty-five years now since they were written, letters from a great Christian woman in Pomerania, written to my fiancée during my imprisonment and, after my release, also to me.

On 20th November 1936 she writes: 'Is it not strange that people at our time should speak of the emptied Word of God. I mean religious people for whom the whole weight and rigour of this "Word" is too heavy, and who would prefer it mild, edifying and soothing. And I, an old woman, realize that in my whole life that "Word" has never been so filled as now; that it is spoken differently and heard differently wherever one asks about it; that an asking of questions arises. May God keep you and all you love. Be assured that all of us will greatly benefit from these tribulations, because in them God loves us.' Is this not Frau von Kleist, as she is portrayed above?

A week later: 'Is it not just in such a time that we grasp fully what it means to have community with one another? Like you I feel that, amidst many sorrows, also of a personal kind, I may sing hymns of praise because life, which seemed to be dead for so long, has become alive. For a person as old as I am this is a special blessing. The absurdity of this life – as seen in the light of what is provisional – loses its sting. The certainty that God holds everything in his hand – really everything – is the mighty comfort, also in face of what men do to us. How strange is the warning of the psalmist: "Do not rely on men." It is so natural that we are always inclined to do it and thus come to grief.'

Again and again she speaks about the great experience of the awakening congregation which, however much she shared the suffering of others and had to bear personal sorrow, was her great joy: 'We live in strange times, and yet we have to give thanks again and again that poor suppressed Christianity is becoming so alive in calamity, as I have never experienced in my seventy years. What a proof of its reality! For more than forty years I have been anxious about the petrifaction of the Church. Oh, it had to happen that it should remember its commission afresh. And Christianity means suffering. But suffering is victory in faith' (24th February 1937).

How much that noble Christian from Pomerania took part in the spiritual life of the Confessing Church, we are told in a note from 17th April 1937: 'This year I have celebrated a wonderful Eastertide in my little country house, because Bonhoeffer and Bethge were with me for twelve days. The former wanted a quiet place where he could work at a book on Christian discipleship. What it meant for me I can hardly express in words. We have often spoken of you and W. and, in our evening prayers, included him in our intercession. This is done every day, also, I know, in Finkenwalde. I am certain that God will hear our prayers. Only His time is not our time. And yet there is always a meaning in it. It is always like this: They meant to deal wickedly with me, but God meant to deal kindly. It strikes me just now how much, and how long, men of the Bible have had to wait. There is something special about such waiting, I think.'

In another letter she mentions Niemöller beside Bonhoeffer: 'God's times are different from ours. The sorrow which has come over our beloved Church and its best men lies heavy on us and many others. Now we must keep the faith. W.'s former chief [Bonhoeffer] recently wrote me: "If one day our work is taken out of our hands, then we must know that God has meanwhile chosen others who step into our places. All that is not for us to decide." I esteem him highly and am grateful for his life. As to our dear Niemöller, I believe that his arrest will prove to be a double-edged sword which does not only strike those who love and venerate him. How many prayers for him must rise to God! For he is beloved up and down the land. His communicants of last year too are dearly attached to him. This U-boat captain who risked his life so often and did so many brave deeds . . .' (7th July 1937).

Another letter confirms that her biblical exegesis for her grandchildren is continuing: 'Wonderful thoughts come into my mind when I reflect on what is happening. Almost all my best friends are suffering. . . . I am now reading the Acts with my grandchildren. What parallels! I hope your Werner has his Bible with him. I keep thinking of this' (19th August 1937).

The extensive material support given to Finkenwalde finds an occasional expression in her letters. Thus, on 8th November 1937: 'Our dear seminary has still no certainty of its final fate. I share these worries with all my heart.' And on 2nd January 1938, after the Team Curacy had been established: 'Christmas has passed without a greeting from me to you. It was a turbulent time for me, also through the fate of our mutual friends to whom I had once been able to offer help and asylum. At some distance from here they have found a new possibility for work, in a changed form. It is very uncertain whether they may continue there. Thus from day to day they live in dependence on divine protection. "Tomorrow will be anxious for itself." I was able to send your letter on to its recipient [Bonhoeffer]. For many weeks he lived in Berlin with his parents, unemployed. But now he can work again, thank God!' And in the same letter: 'I have read a book by Bonhoeffer, *The Cost of Discipleship*. This is a very great gift for me, because it answers the questions I have been asking for decades. And though it contains difficult passages, it is quite comprehensible for the non-theologian who has some training in spiritual things. I am reading it for the second time and shall read it often again, to get it quite clear. . . . When I went to see Frau Niemöller last November she told me that her husband had said to her: "Let us quite consciously give up all waiting and leave it entirely in God's hands." Then he looked at her and added: "Be of good cheer. The thing is worth it."'

When Niemöller was sent to the concentration camp of Sachsenhausen, she wrote (4th March 1938): 'I hear that N. has been taken to S. where Koch was. . . . Oh, my heart is sore for the one and the other.' And ten days later: 'The misery of it all rushes upon me, again and again. For all of us this situation is a trial of faith in which we have to win through to complete obedience, again and again. Only let us not grow feeble in prayer. It is the only help for us and ours.' And on 29th March 1938: 'The three pastors in concentration camps are the subject of my constant intercession. Recently I read John xix, 11, from the Finkenwalde order of meditation. We must think of that, always. I can no longer pray: Deliver them, for I believe that God knows how ardently we wish for this but leaves them there on purpose. But I pray: Give them the strength so to bear everything that they can say: In all this, we fully overcome – so fully that they no longer feel any sufferings because Jesus is standing beside them and bears them himself.'

After I was released from the concentration camp, there were two letters of the 8th and 11th December 1938: 'What can I say? I am overwhelmed with joy about the good news. Yes, let us praise the name of the Lord together. Men believe that it is they who act, but God laughs at them,' and 'My granddaughter wrote today: "I am not able yet to grasp that this great burden is suddenly slipping from our shoulders." I have just talked to a young Finkenwalde brother – so much rejoicing everywhere.'

The reader may think to himself: let us hope the writer knows there are other representatives of Pomeranian aristocracy. He does know, and he did not omit to speak about it too with this great lady. She answered on 20th January 1943: 'What you say about the shortcomings of the Prussian aristocracy is entirely in keeping with my own opinion. Too much tradition, too little live faith. That could not last in time of trial. It is an experience which always makes me very unhappy. . . . And yet it is nonsensical to think that this or that quality could be preserved. In every individual case tradition must be filled with living faith. But where do I lose myself. . . . "All have sinned and fall short of the glory of God."' And in the same letter, at the time when the battle of Stalingrad was lost, there is a hint of how this extraordinary woman faces her own end, taking comfort in faith: 'I think we are going into very hard times. I have lost another grandson, our Max, whom you may remember from earlier times. All the four boys whom I have brought up have been killed in action.' 'One son-in-law and five of my grandsons are in the field, a sixth is due to be called up any day. After the loss of one son-in-law and four grandsons one must pray for a brave heart every day' (3rd June 1943).

After Dietrich Bonhoeffer's arrest she writes (4th November 1943): 'I am glad he has the chance of working. His letters to his parents are truly edifying. More I cannot tell you. In all present need I find comfort in the Word: "I am given all power in heaven and on earth." It is for us to have faith without seeing. With Martin [Niemöller] it is better than before, but unchanged.'

And now the last two letters, with the end in sight; the first is written on 5th August 1944 after the Western front had collapsed: 'You, as well as we here, are dangerously near the theatre of war. It requires a brave heart not to feel troubled. The refugees from East Prussia are arriving here and have saved nothing. But this is not the worst. We ourselves need your intercession because, without any discernible reason, my son with many others of his equals was arrested a fortnight ago and has not been released so far. They are hermetically sealed off and cannot be reached by any letter or visit. It is very hard to know nothing about them and to suffer innocently. My son lived here, in peace, entirely for his numerous and pressing

Bonhoeffer with a group of students at Finkenwalde

The Brethren House

duties. Now it is harvest time, and they have taken him away in the middle of it. We are waiting daily for his return. But as so many thousands have to suffer, we must not complain that we have been hit too. The misery of the whole world is too terrible.'

And now the last news that reached us (26th February 1945): 'Please do not think my silence means disloyalty; it is lack of energy at a time when all words become difficult, and yet so many letters should be written. My eyes begin to fail too. Oh, I have often thought of you and your husband, all the same. I wonder whether my letter will reach you. We are as it were in a mouse-trap. The Russian Army behind us and on all sides, the sea before us, house and village full of refugees so that it is often difficult to manage with the work and the food. But recently we have been so very happy to have my son back after seven months. Just as unceremoniously as your husband once returned. I cannot describe our gratitude. At the same time we feel the greatest anxiety about his nineteen-year-old daughter who was on a visit to Silesia on the other side of the river Oder when the Russian Army suddenly invaded it. We only know that she intended to 'trek' the next day with her friend and her friend's mother. But meanwhile five and a half weeks have passed and no news. How God tries us! Four of the landowners I knew in the Neumark have been murdered by the Russians. If the same fate is in store for us we shall take it from the hands of God. . . . But God can build walls around us, and we have received so much help and protection recently that it would be unthinkable not to put our trust in him. Sometimes I think of the sermon your husband preached about Elijah and the ravens and the widow of Sarepta. Oh we must pray for faith. . . . With D. [Dietrich Bonhoeffer] things are worse than before, also with his whole family. I had rather talk to you about this. Eberhard [Bethge, Bonhoeffer's friend] is going the same way but seems to be less endangered. I have not heard anything about Martin [Niemöller]. May God keep you and Werner and the baby and your mother. Ever yours, Ruth von Kleist-Retzow.'

The Russians did come indeed, but nobody suffered harm. God built his walls around Klein-Krössin. Shortly after the arrival of the Russians Frau von Kleist-Retzow, in consequence of a domestic accident, was called to the Lord who was her only comfort in life and in death.

My report is at an end. Whenever I hold in my hand the crumpled driver's licence which was acquired in Finkenwalde, I remember the people I met there. For their sake I, too, say: Unforgettable Pomerania!

# When He Sat Down at the Piano
## JOHANNES GOEBEL

My most precious memories of Bonhoeffer date from the first
course at the Finkenwalde Preachers' Seminary, in which I
took part. I have only dim recollections of one of his lectures
at the University, which I heard when I was an assistant
preacher in Berlin, and of an evening in his parents' home.

Today I know that his course at the seminary gave a decisive
form to my life, though I have not kept up the meditative way
of life and his special style of preaching. On the whole our
natures were different. Yet the Bonhoeffer of *The Cost of
Discipleship* is very near to me, and what he wrote at that time
is of all his works most familiar to me and as it were a formative
image for my own theology and point of view. Hence the
Bonhoeffer of the third period, who provides questions, and
sets limits, and establishes correlations, gives me the way to
solve problems in present-day theology. This holds true even
though I cannot preach as he did.

Here are some of my memories. All the brethren at Finkenwalde helped to reconstruct the boys' school as our seminary.
But as the clumsiest among them I was given the task of allotting
the texts for morning and evening prayers – a task which I
thoroughly enjoyed. Bonhoeffer knew how to appraise the
abilities of each of us, and to make the best of them. He could
do this even with those of a more retiring nature, and those
who were not so close to him. I did not belong to the innermost
circle (which included Bethge, Onnasch, Kanitz and Schönherr),
but I was one of those who just went along. Any opposition to
him would have seemed senseless to me – though there was a
certain quiet resistance – and I was happy to be led by him.

What still impresses me today even in memory was the

eruptive concentration of his nature in preaching, in lecturing, in talks round the table. He was one of the few people in whose presence I found it easy to express unfinished, immature thoughts, hints and the like. He knew how to turn even abstruse ideas into something positive; we felt that and became confident. Had he not told us that even an answer or a question that seemed silly might be of use? It made us happy to experience the same objectivity, but also the concentration peculiar to him, when he listened to our confessions. Now in retrospect it seems to me that he did not come by it easily, that he even forced himself to it. At that time the deliberate self-effacement which he practised in listening to us, but which involved a real and forceful transmission of strength, had an exciting effect on us, compelling us to the last effort, but at the same time liberating and relaxing us. I felt that this man of strong will, so strange to me, understood me all the same, and it would be nonsensical to hide something, not to commit myself.

There is another, different memory. Once I was present when he sat down at the piano. He was improvising. As I like to do that too, I was interested in his playing perhaps more than he thought agreeable or important. I asked him whether he had ever tried, or was trying, to compose anything. In a distinctly reserved tone he said he had stopped doing so since he had become a theologian, or something to the effect. This seems to me a typical trait of his nature. Bonhoeffer was a passionate preacher and theologian, as Bethge confirms. To sit down at an instrument and improvise or even compose – and not just play Mozart with exactitude, as Jochen Kanitz did – this can only be done in passion, and out of passion. Bonhoeffer cast this passion out of his life for the sake of the call to a greater 'passion'. This too is a contribution to the theme of 'Call and Discipleship'.

That it was a 'casting out' is quite clear to me from a picture which rises in my memory, very distinctly, lit up as if by lightning, a scene which cannot be forgotten: while he was

sitting at the piano something which I had not known in him
and have never seen again, an expression of natural force, of
something primeval, came over him, a Dietrich different from
the one known to us. It was not just his natural freshness, his
energy, his will-power. I am reminded of pictures and tales of
Max Reger, when I recall him sitting there at the piano: he
did not sit erect, but slanting to the right, as if thrown, while
normally even his way of sitting betrayed his concentration of
will: he was sitting as a pupil playing the piano would never
have been allowed to sit. And his playing was hard, he ham-
mered away, too loud. I do not, unfortunately, remember the
musical style of his improvisation, probably because it fascinated me more to witness the native human quality breaking
through his personality, than to pay attention to his music.
And suddenly he stopped as abruptly as he had begun.

It is strange that this should have been so preserved by my
memory; this lightening up of a rudimentary 'non-Bonhoeffer',
and after that the short, harsh, sharp overcoming of himself,
in the way he broke off his playing so suddenly, in his answer
to my amiably condescending question implying such a subtle
criticism of my curiosity, in the vigorous turning back to 'work',
to the 'essential Bonhoeffer'. I can only interpret all this as an
overcoming of self which, in principle, had been accomplished
long before. To him this may have been a trifle then, not worth
mentioning. To me it remains a contribution to 'sanctification',
to 'discipleship', and surely as such a precious memory.

# The Single-heartedness of the Provoked
## ALBRECHT SCHÖNHERR

I think it was on a platform of the Stettiner Station in Berlin that I first shook hands with Bonhoeffer, in the summer of 1932. A small group met there to take part in a student reading party in the youth hostel of Prebelow near Rheinsberg, under the leadership of the young Berlin lecturer. I cannot say that all the exercises, prayer meetings, meditations, and singing practice which were demanded of me, a twenty-year-old youngster, captivated me in a place which was ideal for idling and bathing. All the same, since that time I have been under the spell of that man who gave himself so entirely, heart and soul, whether in play or in theological discussion.

What was it that fascinated us young people in Bonhoeffer? Nothing particular: his appearance was imposing but not elegant; his voice high, but not rich; his formulations were laborious, not brilliant. Perhaps it was that here we met a quite single-hearted, or in the words of Matthew vi, 22, a 'sound' man. Never did I discover in him anything low, undisciplined, mean. He could be relaxed, but he never let himself go. It is for such a life of one piece, such an example that a young person longs. Bonhoeffer detested binding men to himself; perhaps for that very reason so many were drawn to him.

A 'sound' life: Bonhoeffer was not a one-sided intellectual. We always felt slightly embarrassed that this townsman, who was moreover five years our senior, proved to be a well-built and trained athlete who simply outran us in all the ball games in Finkenwalde. It is not for nothing that in his baptismal letter from Tegel prison he wished his godson might inherit his leg muscles.

I learned from him what games mean for a community like a preachers' seminary. When Bonhoeffer proposed them, we

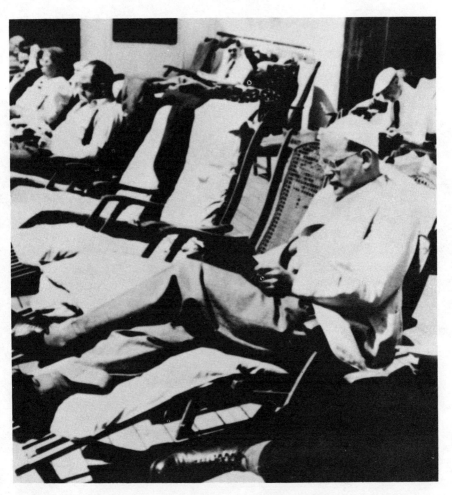
Bonhoeffer on his way to the United States, 1939

young students first turned up our noses. But then we threw ourselves into it because he threw himself wholeheartedly into it. During the second Finkenwalde course we had the good fortune to have two grand pianos in the music-room. The times when Bonhoeffer and a student sat down to play a piano concerto by Beethoven were high-lights in our life together.

From all this we learned that the asceticism of the daily morning and evening devotions (each lasted about forty-five minutes and consisted, apart from one free prayer, of readings of texts and singing of hymns), the half-hour of meditation, the time of silence after getting up and before going to bed – that all this was not due to a toying with monkish habits, or to an aestheticizing liturgism, or the desire to apply psychological leading strings; but to the innermost concentration on the service for which he prepared us, and for which he lived. A unifying arch swung from music and play to quietude and prayer, from the exciting sobriety of his lecture on 'Discipleship' to the Finkenwalde rule: Never speak about a brother who is absent.

A sound life: Bonhoeffer had nothing of the discontinuity of modern man. He had a clear connection with the past. His relation to his mother was filled with deep veneration. His father formed him in his way of thinking. If you come from a large family yourself, you remember a little painfully what he told you of his parents' house: even the children were forbidden just to chatter. Each word mattered and was weighed. One incident is characteristic. One of the family asked what kind of person might be considered as 'clever'. Without a moment's reflection Bonhoeffer's father answered: 'He is clever who knows his limitations.'

Bonhoeffer spoke with great respect of his teacher, Adolf Harnack. Harnack, together with Ricarda Huch, delighted in assembling in his house the numerous scholars who at that time lived in the Grunewald district of Berlin. The procedure on those evenings was that Harnack raised a problem and expected each guest to contribute to the discussion from his own standpoint.

Bonhoeffer, then a sixth-form pupil, was also invited, and it is in-
dicative of Harnack's liberal way of thinking that the judgement
of the grammar-school boy was heard with the utmost attention.

A sound life: Bonhoeffer's personality expressed itself most
directly and most vividly when he was entirely concentrating
on something. He hated to make a psychological effect. He
liked to keep his distance, and he did not permit any undue
familiarity. He did not conceal his middle-class background.
He was able to accept others. In the seminary, for instance, he
approved of trial sermons if they were good, though they might
be very different from the way he would have composed them.
I sometimes suffered a little from his lack of direct personal
warmth. I know, however, that he took great trouble with those
who were in real spiritual need, had endless discussions with
them and was ready to help them to the point of self-sacrifice.

In his sermons he avoided any rhetorical effect. He never gave
us anecdotes in them. He chose the most sober, matter-of-fact
form, the homily. In spite of this, or perhaps because of it, they
were extraordinarily impressive. There was not a word too
many. Only the matter itself came to speech, sometimes in such
a compressed way that what he had to say seemed almost forced
out. It may be typical of Bonhoeffer's way of preaching that
today, after thirty years, his texts still cling in the memory,
whereas the pattern of thoughts has gone.

A sound life: Bonhoeffer possessed what our Church as a
whole and we Christians in particular lack so much. He willed
what he thought. And he thought sharply, logically. This was
sometimes inconvenient even to the brethren of the Confessing
Church. His thesis 'He who deliberately separates himself from
the Confessing Church in Germany, separates himself from
salvation' (in 'The Question of the Community of the Churches',
1936) was not understood even by his theological friends. I
shall not forget the moment when we heard the news, so fateful
for the Confessing Church, especially in Pomerania, that the
State had formed church committees from both camps to bring

Dietrich Bonhoeffer in about 1931

about a pacification of the Church struggle. The postman had just delivered the newspaper. We were still standing on the stairs. Bonhoeffer thought it over for a few seconds, then he was quite clear about it: 'Church and un-church cannot come to terms.' From that moment there was no hesitation. One of the students who had submitted to the church committees was sent away by us, in great distress, but also, after everything had been clarified, with great calmness.

During the initial phase of the Church struggle Bonhoeffer learned that one of the people, who was later to become prominent in the Confessing Church, wondered if he should join the German Christians in order to break that movement from inside. Immediately Bonhoeffer went to see him, accompanied by a few young friends. The illustration which Bonhoeffer then used in his argument has since been very helpful to me in similar situations: 'If you board the wrong train it is no use running along the corridor in the opposite direction.'

Bonhoeffer believed that his political responsibility, too, belonged to the wholeness of life which he owed to his Lord. He was one of the very few people who, as early as January 1933, saw with absolute clarity what was happening. He knew that Hitler's government meant war, and he was astonished that the Allied powers did not strike at the moment when Germany began to rearm. From 1934 we shared his anxiety, year after year, that war might break out – most of all in March 1936 when Hitler reoccupied the Rhineland. War did come three years and six months later, dictated in its first phase by an unparalleled military power.

This is part of his 'sound' life too; this theologian and Christian had become more and more clearly convinced that the substance of God's actions and the substance of man's responsibility for his fellow-men was the idea of deputyship; he therefore staked his life for the liberation of Germany and the world from the curse of murderous tyranny. When, during the war, I saw him for the last time, he was quite bound in the freedom of this responsibility.

# Something Always Occurred to Him
## WILHELM ROTT

I saw Dietrich Bonhoeffer for the first time in Bonn, during the summer semester of 1931. The young scholar had returned from the United States and wanted to meet Barth. In the two seminars we were busy with Schleiermacher. There and in the small group of the master's 'Society' which met in his private study, we witnessed his joy in discovery and the art of his interpretation, though he was still regarded as the furious liquidator of the 'Church father of the nineteenth century'. We read the *Brief Outline of Theological Studies*, and even now, after decades, I recall the delight with which Barth dealt with the famous ninth paragraph: 'If we envisage the union of religious interest and a scholarly mind, both of the highest degree, and distributed in as even a balance as possible over theory and practice: then this is the idea of a prince of the Church.'

During his two weeks in Bonn Dietrich Bonhoeffer took part in Barth's 'Society', and followed it up by one of his *privatissima* with Barth. Whether it was the evening of the ninth paragraph, I forget. But for me, the appearance of Bonhoeffer in Bonn and the 'idea of a prince of the Church' belong together, and I could well imagine a biography of Bonhoeffer as a commentary – and surely a critical commentary – on Schleiermacher's vision, especially if we do not overlook the elucidation in small print given by Professor Schleiermacher (who had just been called from his Stolp parish to the chair in Halle): 'Such a fixation for the theological ideal . . . does not in the least imply a special official position.'

Some years later we talked about how things would have turned out had it not been for the year 1933. Dietrich said: 'Well, I might have been called to Giessen (like Harnack), and then perhaps to a larger faculty; but what I am allowed to do now is far better: all the possibilities of direct moulding in a persecuted church!' – 'Theory and Practice' – 'He who *does* what is true comes to the light' (John iii, 21) – how Bonhoeffer loved these words.

Bonhoeffer as a 'prince of the Church' – an almost amusing idea if we do not remember what else Schleiermacher has to say in this context, especially about 'church rule'. Bonhoeffer did not belong to any authoritative committee of the Confessing Church, but the highly aristocratic Pomeranian Brethren's Council knew how to appreciate this abbot without mitre and crozier. We all shared in Bonhoeffer's pleasure when the Council congratulated him officially and solemnly on his thirtieth birthday and expressed their gratitude towards their adviser and theological expert.

Later in Finkenwalde I realized how unique Bonhoeffer's moulding power was. A young man who was as yet unsettled in his theological convictions could hardly escape this radiating power unless he was a fool. Bonhoeffer knew this. In *Life Together* he makes an over-sharp distinction between communities that are determined psychologically or spiritually, then he withdraws in self-criticism, recognizing the dangers of psychological domination of the other.

I now regret that in Finkenwalde I kept away from the 'Brethren House' members, as I suspected them of fanaticism; but I learned to train myself with lasting profit in biblical meditation, and above all I learned to admire and respect our 'principal's' gift of teaching and his unique success as a teacher. A course in the seminary only lasted a few months, and what Dietrich Bonhoeffer inculcated in the motley crew of students during that time was truly amazing. The thirty-year-old teacher was an all-round man. During the great church visitation of the Confessing Church, which was carried through by brethren of the western provincial churches in East Prussia (in the early summer of 1936), I met my old *Stift* inspector

Professor Horst in Königsberg; when I told him of the activities in Finkenwalde, he said in his sarcastic way: 'They must have found the Nürnberg funnel [the patent method of teaching dullards] in Finkenwalde.' I thought of the classes in the Bonn seminary and laughingly agreed.

Finkenwalde Preachers' Seminary was entirely the child of Dietrich Bonhoeffer, and in the cluster of the five illegal seminaries of the Old Prussian Church it represented something special. Nobody could or would withdraw from the life together, not even the critically-minded inspector of studies, nor the Rhenish student who confided to his countryman: 'Of course it could be done another way.' The same brother made the following remark which so much reflects the political background: 'You are the vice-chancellor, but Eberhard [Bethge] is the representative of the Führer.' I believe that any head of a preachers' seminary today could esteem himself fortunate if he gathered round him a group so joyful and so earnest, unmarried and undistracted. Our situation of course was an unparalleled one, and equally unparalleled were the scholarly qualifications and pastoral passion which were united in Bonhoeffer; that is why Finkenwalde just cannot be imitated. But much of what was worked out and experienced there might be of lasting value for our student communities.

Bonhoeffer was by nature reserved. I was astounded when he told me that beside his relatives he only called one person '*du*'. In the seminary he was addressed as 'Herr Pastor', and soon 'Brother Bonhoeffer'; indeed, the number of the people he called '*du*' soon increased there.

Thus for two years, mostly after lunch and before making the round through the 'halls' of the seminary, 'Brother Dietrich', who always had time for his brethren, sat on the steps of the small stairway which led to the inspector's room. The picture is unforgettable: the small wooden staircase, the man sitting on it with crossed legs, reaching now and then for a cigarette, or accepting a cup of coffee poured out of the only coffee machine of the house. He had been in Berlin yesterday; he told us of it. Late in the evening when he came home, he gave those who waited for him one of his exciting reports about the deviations and embroilments of that time of church committees, about spiritual and worldly affairs, politics of the Church and of the State, about those who stood firm, those who wavered and those who fell. But there was more, there were characteristic details which did not escape the sharp observer, and these could not be told to a large audience. He spoke with great respect of Paul Humburg, the Rhenish *Präses*, which pleased the Rhinelander in the group. Do the Reformed Protestants possibly have more understanding for 'simple obedience' and for discipleship than the Lutherans with their cast-iron doctrine of the two kingdoms? Has the West more understanding for experiments in discipleship to Christ? I had to dampen his optimism considerably. Among my books he discovered those by Geyser and Kohlbrügge; he hardly knew these exegetes, if my memory serves me right. He read them at once: 'Yes, that is how we should stick to the Word.' He was attracted by Kohlbrügge's typological interpretation of the Old Testament. Historico-critical research was a matter of course for him, but it had 'got in his way', and he said: 'The professors accuse me of being unscholarly, because of my biblical work on the Old Testament (in the light of the Church struggle); but they forget that there was genuine exegesis before the new fields of research, the historico-critical and the comparative approach, existed.' Like Karl Barth whose 'every word' he had read, Bonhoeffer approached the texts as a dogmatist and a preacher; the question of method hardly arose at that time. All the same, he was acquainted with the idea and matter of hermeneutics – not every theologian of those times knew the word – he was reading Hofmann's *Hermeneutics*. Bonhoeffer was determined to make the texts speak to our time, including the so-called psalms of vengeance, and for that end every help and every commentator was welcome. Thus Vilmar's *Collegium biblicum* was in high regard with us and probably used more than Lietzmann's *Handbooks* to the New Testament.

From the 'staircase talks' I want to quote two points. We were speaking about the uproar caused by his bold assertion: 'He who deliberately separates himself from the Confessing Church, separates himself from salvation.' It did not seem to affect him. He remarked: 'Once the gunpowder smoke has dissolved, everybody who thinks objectively and dispassionately must agree with me.' But he was glad when he heard that Peter Brunner, after a protest from the Reformed Rhenish general-superintendent, had on the basis of the Lutheran Confession defended and affirmed his provocative thesis in a declaration for the Council of the Rhineland. Another lasting impression made upon me was Bonhoeffer's complaint how much we lacked the 'love of Jesus'. He sought the figure of the humiliated one, of the earthly Jesus, in the Christ of faith, 'with all his heart'. Real faith and love were identical for him. Here was the very heart and core of the existence of this highly intellectual Christian; we felt it in the improvised prayers of the morning and evening devotions; they sprang from the love of the Lord and of his brethren.

Brother Dietrich practised this love of his brethren in many small services at the seminary. The principal liked to play the deacon. Due to the tight budget, the food was simple and in the long run monotonous. Once during a short illness the inspector thought so too but did not say anything. The loving medical orderly, however, realizing the wretched situation, disappeared into the kitchen and soon returned with an opulent breakfast in best English style. 'No rule without exception,' he remarked, laid the small table and vanished once more to brew a strong pot of tea. The meal which they shared made the invalid forget his sickness.

He bestowed this matter-of-course brotherly love on his most beloved brethren, the prisoners. In summer 1936 Pastor Pecyna and Vicar Brandenburg were among the first prisoners. Prayers of intercession were said all the time, and the next Sunday we went off by car to see the prisoners in the Neumark. In autumn 1937 I myself experienced this same love. I was under arrest in Alex and then in Moabit. One day I was taken to the room of the examining magistrate. To my astonishment Dietrich was there. After greeting me he explained he needed from me information about last year's cash balances. I had to turn my thoughts to the potato supplies of Pomeranian junkers, numbers were buzzing through the room, the magistrate plunged into his files, and soon we were able to exchange news. It probably did not escape the *Landgerichtsrat* that we continually switched from numbers to people, though he may not have noticed that by the name Martin (which occurs frequently with theologians) none other than Niemöller was meant, whom I had been happy to see in good shape, a few days ago, in the large building. After my release in late autumn, there was Dietrich again. He had tickets for *Don Giovanni*, and with Eberhard Bethge we celebrated my newly won freedom in the opera house, and after that somewhere else. After hearing my report, Dietrich said something like: You are lucky that time has not hung heavy with you. Other brethren have suffered greatly under their loneliness. It is a great mercy to be surrounded by thoughts and be able to follow them up. 'Horrid [he often used this word] if nothing occurs to you.'

Something always occurred to Dietrich, not only in research and teaching, but also when help for the brethren was needed. Looking back on the year 1937 now, it looks truly harmless compared to what was to darken our world in the forties. The 'ambiguous' Bonhoeffer was untiringly active in trying to save the victims. He and his friends of the Counter Espionage succeeded as late as the end of 1941 in getting a number of Jews into Switzerland. Ever new difficulties and reverses had to be faced. But at last we also managed to have our assistant settled in the train to Basle, with passport, visa, and star of David.

When I came home that evening, my wife told me: 'Bonhoeffer and Dohnanyi have just been here. When they left they said: "This was a great day."'

A few weeks before Dietrich's arrest, at a time when his hands, and those of his friends, were already tied to a large degree, Dietrich invited me to his parents' house to discuss my professional and personal situation. 'We have to try and keep you here in action as long as possible.' (I was then the only member of the Provisional Church Government who was still free.) But how? Those of the Canaris Office who were in the secret had already been checkmated and no longer had any access to their chief. After some reflection it occurred to Dietrich to engage the help of a woman known to both of us. This saving angel was the deaconess Hanna Reichmuth of Schlachtensee, an active member of the Confessing Church. In the darkness of that very night she carried a few words of information to the Villa Canaris, and the admiral reacted immediately. In the summer of 1943, however, I had to exchange my service in the government of the Confessing Church for service in the Army, and after the capitulation I was automatically arrested, as a member of the Counter Espionage, and put in Moosburg Camp.

In this camp, which was for a long time hermetically sealed off from the outside world, the news of Bonhoeffer's death reached me in the middle of summer 1945. A Munich banker, who had belonged to the group round Prelate Neuhäusler and Dr. Josef Müller, got leave of absence for a day. Dr. Müller had known about my relation with Bonhoeffer, so I asked the banker to inquire about Dietrich's fate. After his return we met in the camp road. 'Do not get a shock: Bonhoeffer is dead, murdered by the SS in the last lap.' I needed some time till I was able to hand on the news to the imprisoned brethren in the large camp. None among the many thousands, not even those connected with the Church, knew his name, and this made me realize in what secrecy the things which had been so central to our lives had happened in the Third Reich. But then we experienced in this very camp that the blood of the martyrs is the seed of the Church; not if we adorn the prophets' graves, but if by their witness we are called to him whose community our brother Dietrich sought 'in discipline and in action and in suffering', and in which he has found eternal freedom.

# The Way of Obedience
## HELMUT GOLLWITZER

In autumn 1946, when we received our first mail in the Soviet prisoner-of-war camps, Gertrud Staewen wrote me on a postcard that Friedrich Justus Perels and Dietrich Bonhoeffer were among the last victims of the great murders. Sobbing with grief I rushed into the forest. Since that time the images of those two have been living in my mind with a heightened intensity. It is all the more strange that I hardly remember any details, especially from my conversations with Dietrich Bonhoeffer. Therefore I can to my great regret contribute very little to evoking his rich and unforgettable personality for those who never knew him.

In the summer term of 1931 a group of Berlin students of theology appeared in Bonn. They told us of a new theological star in far-away Berlin, named Dietrich Bonhoeffer, a young lecturer to whom they were deeply attached as teacher and leader. We, select little groups assembled round the thrones of our respective masters in Bonn and Marburg, and full of priggishness, heard such reports with scepticism. What good could be expected from Berlin in the field of theology at that time? Then Dietrich Bonhoeffer came to Bonn for discussions with Karl Barth, and in my digs he and those Berlin students met with their newly-won Bonn friends. Bonhoeffer tells us of this meeting in the letter which reports about his visit to Bonn (GS I, pp. 18 ff.). Winfried Maechler, Wolfgang Schrader, Barbara Damaschke, the daughter of Adolf Damaschke, who is now in East Berlin as the wife of a superintendent, belonged to that group. I do not recall what it was we discussed with Bonhoeffer, but it must have been the relation between theology and philosophy, a problem which in connection with the question of natural theology agitated us greatly. We spoke the lofty language of the early Heidegger – at least some of us, including myself – and harboured a special mistrust of Bonhoeffer, as it had come to our knowledge that in his Christology he leant on the christological views of Hegel. This rumour seems unfounded when compared with Bonhoeffer's texts of that time as published today, especially his lectures on Christology. Its cause was presumably Bonhoeffer's seminar on Hegel's Christology which he held when he was a young lecturer in Berlin. The dissertation of his friend Franz Hildebrandt, 'Est, the Lutheran Principle' shows the influence of Hegel's thought much more strongly than do the writings of the early Bonhoeffer.

We became friends through the Church struggle, which often brought us together. In autumn 1937, after seven weeks in prison, I was invited by Dörthe Kögel, the widow of the Greifswald New Testament professor Julius Kögel, and her sister Hanna von Nathusius, to recover in her house (which was part of the Neinstedt Institutions founded by her grandfather). There Hans Asmussen picked me up for a glorious drive to the Brocken, of which I mainly remember our incessant singing of hymns. We kept it up the whole way through the Harz Mountains. The drive ended in the Bonhoeffer holiday home in the Harz. In my memory, I still see us sitting on their terrace and looking across the sunlit meadow, a happy group of friends, talking with the untrammelled gaiety which was possible to us at that time. It must have been on the same afternoon that we discussed the meaning of the Lutheran doctrine of communion in our time – we were just then preparing for the Confessing Synod of Halle. It struck me that Bonhoeffer was more strongly convinced than I was that the Lutheran exegesis of the sacramental words could be upheld even today. We agreed, however, that the difference between the Lutheran and Reformed traditions of the doctrine of the sacraments could no longer be divisive.

I had similar talks with Bonhoeffer as those Gerhard von Rad describes, and in the same years. We had made a fresh discovery of the Old Testament as a book of the Christian Church. The necessity of warding off the attacks against the Old Testament, and of opposing the 'de-judaizing' of Christianity, had led us all the more deeply into a knowledge of the Old Testament, just as the use of the psalms and the direct and actual meaning of Old Testament statements and stories for our situation had already done. Hans Hellbardt's exegesis of Israel's entering into the land as a parallel to the confessional questions of our time, and to the relation between the churches which were still intact and the Brethren's Councils ('Confessio transjordanea' in *Theologische Aufsätze zu Karl Barths 50. Geburtstag* 1936, pp. 164 ff.), was an example for us of the relevance of the Old Testament. We were doubtless in danger of running into a fundamentalism which simply ignored the achievements of historico-critical research, and equally into an allegorism which saw, in parallels like those drawn by Hellbardt, the essential meaning of the Old Testament. The criticisms of Schlatter, Baumgärtel and Gerhard von Rad excited us greatly, but in our youthful pride we dismissed them as being a matter for the older generation who were not able to overcome their liberal and rationalistic presuppositions. Our fundamentalism, so it seemed to us, held the future. Starting his exegesis of the Old Testament from this point, Dietrich Bonhoeffer found a message for our situation, but in my opinion his theological basis was undoubtedly wrong, when he thought he could interpret the Christian meaning, say of Ezra and Nehemiah, direct from the text, ignoring its historicity. I presume this was the 'positivism of revelation' which in his letters from prison he thought he found in Barth. With this reproach he does not really touch Barth, but rather his own earlier period, that is to say, what he understood and accepted in the thirties as the anti-liberal theological trend of Barthian theology.

As a young pastor of the Confessing Church I had to take the place of Martin Niemöller in the Dahlem congregation. I got into trouble through a conflict with the elders who, led by a pastor who had changed over from the Confessing Church to the Consistory (Church Administration) and the 'middle party', wanted to reduce my activity in the congregation as far as possible. For certain reasons I expected help through the intervention of Fritz von Bodelschwingh and Dietrich Bonhoeffer. In two lengthy evening conversations I explained the whole miserable situation to Bonhoeffer, who to my annoyance listened to it all with equanimity. Our tempers were too different. I flew into a passion, and was mortified that he seemed too phlegmatic. Tall, strong, and in undisturbed calmness he sat there, and with his fair, bright face (which according to the current doctrine of race would have been classified as 'Westphalian') he gazed at me attentively, but showed little response. He expressed resignation about the people with whom I asked him to use his influence, and exhorted me to be patient. Only gradually did I realize that he had assessed the situation with a better judgement of people than I; that he had shown more sense in urging me to be patient than in making illusory promises.

In my desire to force him along the way I wanted in this matter, I brought every available weapon into the field, including his own much disputed thesis: 'He who deliberately separates himself from the Confessing Church, separates himself from salvation.' We discussed this assertion, its justification and its limits, more than once. Its peremptory nature and the decision to which it was intended to summon us ran counter to my mediating nature. In one of the first conversations I had had with Martin Niemöller in the early years of the Church struggle, he had emphasized that the real frontier was not so much between the German Christians and the rest of the Church, as between the Confessing Church and the middle party. Now to my mind the unavoidable consequence of those two views, of Niemöller and Bonhoeffer, was the transition to the Free Church, and as I feared the sectarian climate of such shut-off confessional groups, I was opposed to these views. Only with time did I learn that what they did not contain was a programme of organization, a glorification of the Free Church over against the People's Church; that they were not meant to have a programme, but indicated the determination with which we had to recognize and stand by the task of the Church, and the relentlessness with which we had to call the other members and servants of the Church to this task.

What I wrote about the way of the Confessing Church in those years was decisively influenced by the talks with Bonhoeffer. Above all he helped and counselled me in a personal question – whether the so-called 'illegal' young pastors and curates who were under the authority of the Brethren's Councils, should submit to the Consistories. This question was pressing indeed. Not so much because we were paid a mere pittance on which some of the young married brethren could hardly exist with their families; but mainly because the Gestapo had threatened to regard us as unemployed and call us up for the construction of the West Wall unless we were recognized by the Consistories as clergymen belonging to the territorial church. In the end some of us were in fact called up to work at the West Wall. A further very urgent reason, which seduced some to arbitrary defection to the Consistory side, was the lack of pastors there and the unprovided-for congregations, to which we otherwise had no admittance.

Entangled as we were in the struggle about the claim of the Brethren's Councils for church leadership, we felt hampered in the more important tasks of proclamation, and found it hard to resist the question whether the fight of the Confessing Church was not being bogged down in a sterile tug-of-war between Brethren's Councils and Consistories. The constant consultations with Friedrich Justus Perels, Hermann Ehlers, Wilhelm Niesel and Dietrich Bonhoeffer were for me a necessary reaffirmation of the conviction that we cannot choose our way, and that we cannot relinquish the way of obedience even if more plentiful fruits seem to beckon from other ways. Here it was mainly Bonhoeffer who knew how to uncover the spiritual core of the problem, which according to the arguments of the other side were a mere matter of Church law. To this day his Finkenwalde community is indebted to him for this spiritual insight.

The Church struggle laid bare a good deal of inner disorder in the pastors. In our search for its causes, and for possible cures, we looked, more thoroughly than at any time since the Reformation, to the orders of the Roman Catholic Church. We felt that the complete elimination of monasticism at the Reformation had been a doubtful step, and, indeed, a great loss. None of us then knew anything of Taizé. But our ideas went in the same direction. It was mainly Bonhoeffer who again and again in his conversations evoked the vision of a religious order living in voluntary celibacy. This vision is expressed in the work he did in the Preachers' Seminary, and in his book on *Life Together*. It was all the more surprising, and also important for me, when in a specially catholicizing period of my development, as I deplored the loss of monasticism as a particular defect of Protestantism, he once described to me the dangers threatening every religious order, and warned me against harbouring the illusion that with the recovery of religious orders in the realm of our Church, a recipe was given for the renewal of the Church.

In the summer of 1951 I stayed in my native country of the Upper Palatinate and visited the ruins of Flossenbürg castle, which has been dear to me since my childhood. When I visited the remnants of the notorious Flossenbürg concentration camp I noticed that there was nothing there, or in the local village church, to remind one of Dietrich Bonhoeffer and his martyr's death. During the following months a commemorative tablet was being discussed, and the question was raised whether Bonhoeffer had really died as a martyr of his faith or only for his political convictions. The commemorative tablet in the Flossenbürg church is the result of those discussions. The distinction which was made in the form of this question would not have been a possible one for Bonhoeffer. The question whether the resistance of the Confessing Church must carry the consequence of political resistance, had been the subject of innumerable discussions both before and after the war had begun. We speedily recognized – at least in the inner circle of our friends – that there could be no separation between the two forms of resistance. The only question which was not decided was whether Church officials, that is, we pastors, should be connected with the political resistance and should co-operate with the resistance groups. In the last conversation that I had with Bonhoeffer we were not entirely of one mind. Just before this conversation took place I had, though with the expression of my greatest sympathy, declined to enter into contact with a left-wing resistance group where communists and socialists worked together. I had given the reason that my work as a pastor of the Confessing Church must remain free of the suspicion that it was motivated by political convictions. Bonhoeffer doubted whether it was right and even possible for us to retain this attitude in the long run. We know how he answered this question for himself. His last years were a protest against the distinction between political resistance and the resistance of the Church. However, he only took an active part in the political resistance after his work in the Church had come to an end, for external reasons. For me too the question in how far the special task of the pastor binds him to restrain himself politically, was soon pushed aside by external factors: I was expelled from the Dahlem congregation and called up to the army. Since then our more intimate circle of friends has never again wavered in its clear affirmation that political resistance, under such a government of murderers, is a consequence of being a Christian, a fruit of faith, and a subject of pastoral counselling.

# From Keelson to Principal of a Seminary
## WILHELM NIESEL

One afternoon in 1918 or 1919 the rowing club of the Fried-richs–Werder Grammar School had one of their outings, starting from their boat-house at the Kleine Wannsee. Most of the boats had landed at Kohlhasenbrück where we planned to have coffee in a garden restaurant near the shore. Belatedly another boat arrived, a two-man boat. Behind the helmsman we saw the 'keelson', a fat boy in a white sweater. When the boat laid alongside the landing-place something happened which we had never experienced before: the boat capsized and the crew fell into the water. The little heap in the white sweater soon emerged again, and turned out to be Dietrich Bonhoeffer. He was too young to be a member of our rowing club but had been invited by friends, and in his inexperience had probably caused that strange spectacle while trying to get out. In my class the name of Bonhoeffer was well known. Our master had an ex-ceedingly high opinion of one of Dietrich's elder brothers, who had been killed in action. Once we even had to write an essay on one of his utterances, which did not particularly thrill us, but was sufficient to engrave the name of Bonhoeffer on our memories. I had no idea that one day I would work in close collaboration with Dietrich Bonhoeffer.

Around the end of 1934 the Council of the Evangelical Church of the Old Prussian Union considered setting up a preachers' seminary for the church province of Berlin-Branden-burg. One day the President of the Berlin Brethren's Council, Gerhard Jacobi, came to see us and pressed upon us the name of Dietrich Bonhoeffer for the post of principal of this seminary. He had, so he said, been profoundly influenced by Gandhi, and this could be of great use in shaping such a community. We were somewhat surprised at this reason, but we knew that Bonhoeffer was a good theologian. I had reviewed his *Sanctorum Communio* a few years earlier, and as a consequence he had sent me his second book *Act and Being* with a friendly note. We found a home for the newly-founded Preachers' Seminary in a vacant building, formerly a privately run boys' school, at Finkenwalde near Stettin. The house was quite neglected, a veritable pigsty. But the young team managed to clean it up and make it habitable with odds and ends of furniture. The five preachers' seminaries of the Confessing Church of the Old Prussian Union were part of my domain, so I soon paid a visit to Finkenwalde and shared for a day in its community of learning and living. Bonhoeffer gave a forthright lecture on 'Life Together', and it astonished me by the dryness of its style and effect. In the discussion that followed I raised the question whether, with such a comprehensive concentration on spiritual things, the candidates had any time for the cinema. I was suspicious of too much 'spiritualism'. In the afternoon we rowed on the lake and recalled the accident at Kohlhasenbrück and its happy end. On the shore we climbed a small hill from where we overlooked the runways of a near-by air squadron, and all the time fighter planes were taking off and landing. There too a young generation was in training, but for a kingdom which had even then begun to reveal its hardness and cruelty. A few months later the third Confessing Synod of the Old Prussion Union was meeting in Berlin-Steglitz, and Dietrich Bonhoeffer felt the pressing need to come and urge us to issue a declaration about the public treatment of the Jewish question. He could not win the President of the Synod over, so that the only decision taken was to refer the matter to the *Reich* Brethren's Council.

Through his relatives Bonhoeffer was in touch with the military *Abwehr* (Counter Espionage). Through this channel the government of the Confessing Church received information about many things that even the highest State offices were ignorant of. Thus we were told beforehand of the exact day when Hitler was to attack Poland and start the war. He was unbelievably successful and surprised all of us by even taking Paris. As it happened we, that is, the Old Prussian Brethren's Council, were meeting a few days later at the house of Pastor Hasse in Nowawes, and during that meeting Dietrich Bonhoeffer breezed in. To our utter amazement he made a speech telling us we had to change our attitude towards Hitler; events had proved that God was with him and we had to recognize it.[1] His arguments did not impress the Old Prussian Brethren's Council, but the triumph of the Prince of this World discouraged us very much. I mention this incident for two reasons: firstly it shows that even the leaders of the Confessing Church were no 'saints'. Also, it demonstrates how violently Bonhoeffer was stirred and sometimes overwhelmed by events. Therefore reflections which he later noted down under the influence of imprisonment should not be looked upon as the basis of a new theology. After those dark weeks of the summer of 1940 Bonhoeffer quickly pulled himself together. If he had lived to see how his letters from prison are sometimes interpreted he might be very critical.

In view of the National Socialist crimes the Old Prussian Brethren's Council faced the problem, in the middle of war,

---

[1] A very different interpretation of this incident is given by Eberhard Bethge in his biography: 'A capitulation of Bonhoeffer, even for seconds, is out of the question. Something quite different happened to him. He wanted to make clear the significance and relevance of the fact that a successful tyranny was apparently going to last longer than they had all thought. Incidentally the contrast for Bonhoeffer between recent hopes that the régime would soon end, and its actual consolidation was far sharper than for his hearers who did not know as much as he did. Since the 17th June Bonhoeffer saw sorrowfully but clearly that there would never again be just a return to what had once been. . . . After the last events, the road to something new would be far costlier and lengthier than they had assumed, and the shape of the goal was yet unknown.' To prove this, Bethge adds sentences from the section 'The Successful Man' which Bonhoeffer wrote a few weeks later, in September 1940, for his *Ethics*. [Note added by the German publisher.]

how to preach the ten commandments to our people aright. A committee was formed consisting of Paul Graf York, Hammelsbeck, Harder, Perels and Bonhoeffer. It was within this group which met from August 1942 to March 1943, mostly in Magdeburg, that I felt nearest to Bonhoeffer. He prepared for us a paper on the *Primus usus legis*, that is on the question of the importance of divine law for public life. He probably never heard of the effect this work produced. The last Old Prussian Confessing Synod, which met in Breslau on 16th and 17th October 1943, approved an exposition of the commandment 'Thou shalt not kill', as well as a statement on the ten commandments, which were to be read from all pulpits. These documents, which included a clear declaration of our sins, were read from the pulpits on the Day of Penitence.

By that time Dietrich Bonhoeffer had been in Tegel prison for more than six months. When Hans von Dohnanyi was arrested and his office searched, a piece of paper was found on which Bonhoeffer had written something concerning myself. It was a request to Dohnanyi to prevent my being called up – though my name was of course not mentioned – so that I might be able to continue serving the government of the Confessing Church. This piece of paper was one of the causes for Bonhoeffer's arrest. Many months later I had news from him. He sent me a secret warning which our common friend, Justus Perels, immediately brought to me in my exile in Lippe. Thus even in prison he did not forget us, but stood up for us as long as he could.

# A Visit at Asparagus Time
## WOLFGANG SCHRADER

We old Finkenwalders were scattered across the country, often holding rather lonely posts. Almost all of us illegal pastors and curates of the Confessing Church were liable to encounter the hostility of the Nazi Party and the Gestapo. Whenever he could, Dietrich Bonhoeffer visited his brethren and urged us in our turn not to leave anybody to himself in his loneliness. Once, in the summer of 1936, he came to see me in Kuhz in the Ucker-mark. He brought Brother Lerche along in his car. It was asparagus time, and as I was still unmarried, I got the local inn to cook a great quantity of the finest, thickest asparagus from my garden and serve it with butter. With it we had boiled potatoes and fresh sliced smoked gammon. It was a delight to see how Dietrich Bonhoeffer happily helped himself and enjoyed the tender asparagus – but without potatoes. He could be so modest in what he required, but he was also able to relish good things to his heart's content. In the afternoon he inquired in detail about the congregation and myself. After that, as far as I remember, we went swimming in the big Kuhzer lake. Then we prepared the evening service to which I had invited the congregation days before. We divided the proclamation among the three of us in such a way that each preached for five minutes. After that, standing in front of the altar of the 700-year-old church built of field stones, we sang in harmony 'The light of the sun has now gone down'. In the evening our guests left us. But for years the congregation talked about this brotherly visitation, and some of them began to see what brotherhood means.

# When the Synagogues Burnt

## GOTTFRIED MALTUSCH

During the tense days of the year 1938 the seminary of the Confessing Church had already been transferred from Finkenwalde to Köslin in Pomerania. We ordinands lived in a large apartment in the superintendent's house. Dietrich Bonhoeffer was the head of the seminary, and the superintendent's son, Pastor Onnasch, ran the inside work of the seminary, as an inspector of studies. In the late evening of the notorious 'Crystal Night' two members of our seminary suddenly appeared and told us that the synagogue of Köslin was burning. SA men in uniform had prevented the fire-brigade from extinguishing the fire. We were extremely disturbed. Some of us were in favour of our all setting off at once to try and perhaps save something. But then we decided not to go as the fire had advanced too far, and for us to hang around as passive onlookers might have given the impression that we approved. Bonhoeffer was not at home that evening. The next day some of us inspected the scene of the conflagration which was still guarded by SA men. We saw that in fact the whole place was burnt to the ground.

A great discussion now arose among us about this deed, and how to assess it. Meanwhile Dietrich Bonhoeffer had returned. Some of us spoke of the curse which had haunted the Jews since Jesus's death on the cross. Bonhoeffer rejected this with extreme sharpness. We had a very full discussion of Matthew xxvii, 25 and Luke xxiii, 28, as well as Romans ix–xi. He utterly refused to see in the destruction of the synagogues by the Nazis a fulfilment of the curse on the Jews. This, he said, was a case of sheer violence. 'If the synagogues burn today, the churches will be on fire tomorrow.' In this action the godless face of National Socialism had shown itself once again.

## When the Synagogues Burnt

In the afternoon we learnt that there had been a planned action throughout the *Reich*. Nowhere in Pomerania had any resistance to it been attempted. The population hardly talked about it. Everybody had the feeling that a grievous wrong had been done; but nobody dared to say it openly.

# Life Together
## HANS-WERNER JENSEN

While we were staying as seminarists in the old Schlönwitz parsonage, striving for a life together, one of the many things that were taking shape in Bonhoeffer's mind was his little book on *Life Together*. I had the great pleasure of typing the manuscript to his dictation. Today this book may be acquired by anybody. But who still feels concerned about what this young 'Doctor of the church' – and that he was in the truest sense of the word – thought about the individual within the community? Here a psychologist has the courage frankly and realistically to identify the craving of the ego for self-assertion in its struggle with others. The egoism even of pious people could not be exposed more passionately than here.

Thus it was not a naïve but a highly conscious love of the Christian community which drove Dietrich Bonhoeffer to become the father, pastor and neighbour of his seminarists. Because Christ said: 'You know that the rulers of the Gentiles lord it over them . . .; it shall not be so among you' (Matthew xx, 25 ff.), serving his brother became the centre of Bonhoeffer's life. He avoided keeping others in tutelage; he only wanted to help them. Here I have to speak of some personal experiences.

I got appendicitis and was taken to Stolp hospital. Of course into the general ward (third class), as becomes a student of theology. The operation was carried out immediately and I spent the following night in the large ward; to my surprise I was transferred to the private patients' department the next morning. I protested against this arrangement, asking who would finance it? The orderly told me that a good-looking gentleman with glasses had been in that morning declaring he would bear the cost. The stranger can have been no other than Dietrich Bonhoeffer.

Another time we were making our way home after an open evening in Berlin. Bonhoeffer bought the tickets for all of us at the station. When I wanted to repay him, he just answered: 'Money is dirt.' But he was much more concerned about helping our souls than our finances. Many owe it to him that they were able to stand up to the Church struggle with a clear conscience.

At that time the German Christians had carried the day in Schleswig Holstein. The Church government was in the hands of the so-called territorial bishop Adalbert Paulsen and his treasurer Dr. Kinder. Some of us felt they could not accept the *licentia concionandi* from their hands, so we emigrated in various directions, some to Württemberg, some to Bavaria, some like myself to Berlin-Brandenburg. There was still a Confessing Church there.

Everybody nowadays knows that, for Bonhoeffer, the daily meditation was one of the first and foremost tasks of the theologian, and an essential part of this was the psalms. Professor Schniewind of Kiel, by pointing to the prayers of the Baltic martyrs, had started me on the way which in Gross-Schlönwitz led to clarity of conviction: I saw the meaning of the psalms as the prayers of the Church, of the people of God, in the desert. I was happy to learn this in the Preachers' Seminary, for I was able to practise it later in a Gestapo prison. There are still some marginal comments to the psalms in my Bible which date from the Gross-Schlönwitz time, for instance the date, 10th November 1938, the 'Crystal Night', beside Psalm lxxiv, 8: 'They burned all the meeting places of God in the land.'

Dietrich Bonhoeffer was at that time driven by a great inner restlessness, a holy anger. With his Mercedes he raced to Berlin to be with brethren and friends in trouble, and driving back through the night he only arrived in the early hours of the morning in our district, which was still comparatively safe from the Gestapo. During those ugly days we learned to understand – not just human revenge, but the prayer of the so-called psalms of vengeance which give over to God alone the case of the innocent, 'for his name's sake'. It was not apathy and passiveness which Dietrich Bonhoeffer derived from them, but for him prayer was the display of the strongest possible activity.

Once I was frightened by a remark of Bonhoeffer's, perhaps in the way the believers who met St. Paul on his way to Jerusalem foresaw his fetters, his prison and his martyr's death. During an animated conversation we discussed the duty of the theologian to be the guardian of the nation's cultural heritage as well, and this took us further to the theme of freedom. Here Bonhoeffer declared that 'secular freedom too is worth dying for'. I wondered what these words had to do with Christian faith and our task in the Preachers' Seminary. But I have never forgotten them, and their importance does not only lie in their present actuality, as it has always done, but they pledge our nation to gratefulness to a martyr of freedom.

On 9th April 1945 in Flossenbürg, Dietrich Bonhoeffer proved his readiness to stand by this bold word of his. Often at night I am haunted by the picture of our brother Bonhoeffer hanging from the gallows, a victim sacrificed in the struggle for freedom. Recently I had to take the funeral of an old woman who had been killed, defenceless, at the hand of a murderer, and again I felt the oppressive nearness of somebody who had died an unnatural death.

What an example Bonhoeffer set for us in his close attachment to his mother! There was hardly a day when he did not have a long-distance talk with her, across those hundreds of miles to Berlin. I doubt whether he would have been such a pastor to his brethren without this constant readiness to listen to his mother. When our then only son had a fatal accident at the age of one-and-a-half, Dietrich Bonhoeffer wrote us a letter which all through the war I carried with me as a priceless treasure. Every year at Advent he sent out personal greetings to all former seminarists – most of whom were on active service.

Each of those greetings steadied our brotherhood, strengthened
our faith and prepared us for service after the war.

Strengthened our faith: the Gestapo arrested me on account
of a sermon on the Good Samaritan, and there was many a
know-all who condemned as unwise the free confession of faith
in a congregation suppressed in its mind and soul by its local
Nazi leader. When Bonhoeffer was asked about his opinion, he
straightway referred us to 1 Thessalonians v, 19: 'Do not
quench the Spirit.'

In this, as always, he did not allow his practical theology to
be determined by law; he acted in the freedom of the spirit. I
remember a conversation about prayers at table. Shall a
Christian, who is accustomed to pray before and after meals,
also do so in a restaurant, or when he is a guest in a house where
this habit is not practised? Every theologian knows how heated
the discussion about such subjects may become in a preachers'
seminary. Opinions clashed: for the sake of our confession we
ought to pray, especially in such circumstances. No, prayer is
not a confession. Now Bonhoeffer advised us to pray or not to
pray as long as it happened in a 'natural' way, without inhibitions, as it were spontaneously. Only there must be no law about
it; for the law breeds contempt of others, because he who prays
is in constant danger of elevating himself above others.

In this way Bonhoeffer wanted a genuine, natural community
in the Preachers' Seminary, and this community was practised
in play, in walks through the richly wooded and beautiful
district of Pomerania, during evenings spent in listening to
someone reading (*Mozart on his Journey to Prague*), in making
music and singing, and last not least in worship together and
holy communion. He kept entreating us to live together naturally and not to make worship an exception. He rejected all false
and hollow sentiment. This was the main point from which he
criticized the sermons and teachings of his students. And yet
he never forgot that at that time of the Church struggle and
imminent war all of us were under sentence of death.

# Two Recollections
## HELLMUT TRAUB

I met Bonhoeffer for the first time in 1937 or 1938. Helmut Gollwitzer had taken me to Stettin where a few people were to meet for a discussion led by Bonhoeffer. I knew him of course by name. I had been deeply and permanently impressed by his *Communio Sanctorum*, which I still think is his most important scholarly book; and in his exegesis of the creation stories – *Creation and Fall* – I encountered entirely new insights. The chapters of his *Cost of Discipleship* on 'Costly Grace' and 'Call to Discipleship' had moved me deeply; they are undoubtedly among the best things he ever wrote.

But there was something else connected with his name which excited us even more, and that was his attitude towards the Church, which had immensely radical consequences, and was also, in an extraordinary way, a matter of course. For had we not all adopted it? But with him it was brought to its logical conclusion. In his essay which appeared in *Evangelische Theologie* (1936, pp. 214 ff., 405 ff.) Bonhoeffer put the question of the Church in this way: If the Confessing Church is *the* Church, then it follows that *extra ecclesiam nulla salus* ('no salvation outside the Church') with all the inherent consequences of that claim. But the decisive thing was that which he radiated: here was a man who could not 'go against the will of God'. Moreover a certain myth was arising even then about Bonhoeffer and his Finkenwalde Preachers' Seminary. I had already heard about his theological scruples concerning Karl Barth, which were later to crystallize in his verdict of a 'positivism of revelation'. This rather surprised me, as I regarded it as a complete misunderstanding not only of Barth's basic starting-point, but also

of his assertion of the vital necessity for the Church struggle. I
was all the more curious to meet him.

I must confess that Bonhoeffer at first simply disappointed me.
The conversation, like innumerable others at that time, dwelt
on the proper theological and practical understanding of
Romans xiii: 'Let every person be subject to the governing
authorities. For there is no authority except from God.' And
our state was the state of Hitler. Bonhoeffer seemed to me extraordinarily reserved, ready to consider every fresh problem put
to him, taking even the remotest ideas into account. His
conservative nature, his scholarly education and his thoroughness prevented any quick result. He spoke slowly, with some
hesitation, but also with great deliberation. Impatient with the
slow and congested argument in which we did not even share
basic principles, I asked with open annoyance what on earth
we should do now, indeed, had to do, as there was no doubt
that we had to resist in the political field too. The question
remained unanswered. But later Bonhoeffer took me aside. He
assured me emphatically that he had understood me perfectly.
'But then you must be quite logical, quite different, you must
go ahead in quite a different way.' One certainly had to 'arrest
the wheel', he said, but not in an adolescent way, in resentment,
thoughtlessly. I at once realized that what I had taken for
'hesitation' belonged to an entirely different category: we had
to become clear about the situation and what it required, we
had to become responsible and to search for a quite new and
binding form of Christian life: it might best be described with
a word that Bonhoeffer loved: *Zucht* (discipline). However, in
our conversation at that moment I still thought I had to accuse
him of remaining, so to speak, in 'meditation', after I had
expected so much of him. He reproved me for my lack of self-
control. But he also answered me in a positive way by saying
that any meditation and contemplation was only possible,
meaningful and permissible if it was connected with a deliberate
entering into and acting within the world. As far as I remember

he not only used the word 'in and of the world' (*welthaft*) which became very important for me, but he also spoke, in this context, of an active, necessary, overwhelming 'crying aloud'. It is difficult to recall the exact words after such a long time. The notes I took at that time were all destroyed in the tumult of the war. But it has remained clearly fixed in my mind that he directed me towards the world (not away from the Church, but from churchliness), that is, to the way of the prophet. I need not add that during this conversation my disappointment vanished. But though he stressed the necessity to 'arrest the wheel', I had the impression of a certain helplessness in Bonhoeffer.

This had entirely changed in 1939. In the spring, Bonhoeffer had gone to the United States – perhaps that 'helplessness' had been one of the reasons for that journey. Germany was in a state of extreme hopelessness. I was sent to replace Bonhoeffer and assist in the work of his Preachers' Seminary. This was no longer at the old place but had fled from the Gestapo to a small farm (where they reared pigs, I think) called Sigurdshof near Schlawe in Pomerania. Another group was lodged in Superintendent Onnasch's house in Köslin. Sigurdshof was almost an idyll, surrounded by forest, inviting us to concentration and work. There was also a wooden shed in the forest which served as a hide-out during unsolicited visits of the Gestapo. There we tried to give our young curates a further training in theology and confessional works, and led a peaceful life, in contrast to the rest of Pomerania, which in the early summer of 1939 became more and more a great military camp. There were soldiers everywhere. Moreover, we listened regularly to the BBC. We had no doubt that war was imminent. Conscious of this, but quite inadequately in face of what was coming, we tried to prepare our young curates for the fearfully difficult decisions before them. I was happy to know that Bonhoeffer was not in Germany, but safe from the coming reign of terror, and the catastrophe which I was convinced would follow. He must not perish in it. He knew about the resurgence of the Church, about the inner necessity (and not just the external necessity conditioned by the German Christians) of the Confessing Church whose destiny he had helped to shape; the best of liberal theology from Harnack's time, as well as the most recent movement of dialectical theology, were alive in him, and equally so an amazingly extensive general, philosophical, literary and artistic education. His openness and his free and unprejudiced conviction that the Church must undergo a change, renew itself, justified the confidence he enjoyed in foreign churches, especially those of the United States, Britain and the Scandinavian countries. He was practically predestined to rebuild the Protestant church after the débâcle which most certainly was in store for us. (A rebuilding which we imagined differently, however.) Over and above this, and apart from the great danger of his situation, Bonhoeffer was sure to find no mercy, as he was bound to be a conscientious objector. There was no room for him in this present-day Germany, because we believed that *then*, later, we would be in real, deepest need of him; *then* his time would come.

And then one day, after a short message that he was returning, Bonhoeffer stood before us. This was quite unexpected – indeed, there was always something extraordinary about him, even when the circumstances were quite ordinary. I was immediately up in arms, blurting out how could he come back after it had cost so much trouble to get him into safety – safety for us, for our cause; here everything was lost anyway. He very calmly lit a cigarette. Then he said that he had made a mistake in going to America. He did not himself understand now why he had done it. His later messages from prison tell us that he never repented having returned from America. It is this fact – that he abandoned in all clarity many great possibilities for his own development in the free countries, that he returned to dismal slavery and a dark future, but also to his own reality – which gave to everything he told us then a strong and joyful firmness, such as only arises out of realized freedom. He knew he had taken a clear step, though the actualities before him were still quite unclear. He gave us two reasons for his return. First, simply his thought of the Confessing Church, which meant for him all the many young brethren, had not given him any rest. He could not stay away from them, he must not leave them. This meant – and this was the second reason – that he could not watch Germany's fate from outside and have no part in it. The idea of taking an active part in reconstruction later, after the war, was out of the question for him unless he shared in the affliction which was coming over Germany, unless he took a real part, and genuinely shared in its trials. Without this any help, even in the best possible case, would only be help from outside. Only he could help, he said, who would bear what was coming and see it through. I objected, saying did he not realize that all was lost; that whatever happened, hardly one of us would survive? Yes, he saw that in precisely the same way; but for that reason – and this was Bonhoeffer's real answer – each of us had to become quite clear about the fact that he was facing a decision: if he wanted Germany's victory he also wanted the end of its freedom and of Christianity in it. The possibility of freedom for Germany and of Christianity in Germany was only given in its defeat. A victory would destroy the real future. It impressed me greatly that to the goods of freedom and Christianity he added those of education and civilization. And then he named his second reason for coming back, the decisive one, speaking calmly, smoking his cigarette, as if he was not saying anything special: I know what I have chosen.

The next morning, after the quiet time of meditation, Bonhoeffer made us stop work. With his young men he drove to the beach on the Baltic for a bathe. Once again he wanted them to feel the sun, to feel what it is like to be free. Out there on the beach he tried to show us that we had to go a further step, however dimly he himself saw what it involved: to be a Christian in and of the world demonstrating with our existence that the Lord is the Lord in the actual reality of this world. Soon our young men were called up. Dietrich Bonhoeffer, Eberhard Bethge and I tidied up, packed books, nailed up windows: leave-taking from the work of the seminaries of the Confessing Church. When we parted, Bonhoeffer remarked he would at last get down to writing his *Ethics*. He did not. He has been granted to live and die it.

# V

1938    In February, first contacts with Sack, Oster, Canaris and Beck

In September, *Life Together* written in Göttingen; sees his twin sister and her husband, Leibholz, of Göttingen, off abroad

1939    10th March, departure for London; meeting with Bishop George Bell, Reinhold Niebuhr, Leibholz, Visser't Hooft

2nd June, departure for the United States; 27th July, back to Berlin

1940    15th March, end of semester in Köslin and Sigurdshof; two days later Gestapo appears with closing-down orders

In August, conversations with Oster and von Dohnanyi about a reserved occupation in the service of the *Abwehr* (Counter-Espionage)

9th September, forbidden to speak in public and ordered to report to the police; in September and October work at the *Ethics* in Klein-Krössin

30th October, to Munich to be seconded to local *Abwehr*; from 17th November guest of the Benedictine Abbey of Ettal

1941    24th February to 24th March, first journey to Switzerland

29th August to 26th September, second journey to Switzerland

1942    10th to 18th April, journey with Helmut von Moltke to Norway and Stockholm

In May, third journey to Switzerland

30th May–2nd June, to Stockholm to meet Bishop Bell

24th November, visit to Pätzig; engagement to Maria von Wedemeyer

1943  5th April, arrested and house searched, taken to Tegel Prison; Hans von Dohnanyi and Dr. Josef Müller with their wives arrested at the same time

# To America and Back

## REINHOLD NIEBUHR

There are many things that I could say about Dietrich Bonhoeffer when he was a student here, particularly about the
combination of his sophisticated theology and simple piety.
We became very warm friends and I corresponded with him all
the time until his imprisonment. I will tell you one story:

When I was in Britain in April before the war broke out, I
was visited by Bonhoeffer and his brother-in-law in a little
village where I was staying in England. He told me that he had
definite information through his connections with the Army
that war would break out in September, and that he couldn't
support the war, and that some of the members of the Brethren's
Council had suggested to him that it would be well for him to
go to America if this were possible. I immediately cabled to
America and he received an invitation from our seminary to
lecture during the summer semester. I remained in England
during this whole time to give my Gifford Lectures and did
not see him. Shortly after the outbreak of the war I received a
letter from him, written in the garden of the President of our
seminary, Dr. Coffin, in which he said that it was a mistake for
him to come to America, that the Christians of Germany would
have to make a decision between wanting the victory of their
nation, and the death of a Christian civilization, or the defeat
of their nation and the survival of a Christian civilization. You
cannot, he said, remain out of a country when your fellow
Christians face such a momentous issue. He hoped, therefore,
that I would understand why he was going back. I report this
because I think it is remarkably symbolic of the spirit of his life.

# Visits to Geneva
## ADOLF FREUDENBERG

My first acquaintance with Dietrich Bonhoeffer dates from the year 1934 when I was secretary to the legation in the Foreign Office of Germany. In the Department for Culture I had, among other things, to deal with the foreign relations of the churches.

One day the two German pastors in London, Bonhoeffer and Schönberger, came to my office to lodge their common complaint about co-operation with the Foreign Office of the German Evangelical Churches (Bishop Heckel). In contrast to Bonhoeffer, Pastor Schönberger had a close relationship with the National Socialist Party, but he had the rather fantastic idea of detaching the German congregations in foreign countries from the Foreign Office of the Church, that is from Bishop Heckel. During the discussion, Bonhoeffer held back; he obviously thought it more appropriate to let Schönberger take precedence with an unknown civil servant.

In the following years I saw Bonhoeffer only rarely, at a lecture, or at large meetings, as I began to study theology in Bethel in 1935. In March 1939 I came to London as a secretary for refugee problems with the Provisional Ecumenical Council, and as the second pastor of the Lutheran St. George's Church. There I saw Bonhoeffer, at least twice, in the company of the present Berlin superintendent, Dr. Julius Rieger, and Professor Franz Hildebrandt, who is now in the United States.

Bonhoeffer was then at Union Theological Seminary in New York and much troubled by the very difficult decision whether he should stay or return to Germany in view of the threatening war. Pastor Eberhard Bethge has reminded me that in June I wrote to Bonhoeffer recommending him to return. I especially warned him against accepting the post of pastor for refugees in

*166*

New York, as this would render his return to Germany under National Socialist rule impossible. It would be preferable for such an office to be taken by an *émigré* pastor who would not go back to Germany anyway. I understand that Bonhoeffer based his decision to return partly on my letter. In summer 1939 I went to Switzerland and built up the work for refugees with the Provisional Ecumenical Council in Geneva. From 1941 on Bonhoeffer was in Switzerland several times and always came to see the small Ecumenical Council whose general secretary, Dr. W. A. Visser't Hooft, he knew from his former ecumenical activities, and whom, even in the difficult war-time conditions, he met in full mutual trust. I had little to do with political affairs and was moreover frequently absent from Geneva. But I know that Bonhoeffer's missions in Switzerland were viewed with considerable mistrust by some Swiss. For them it was hardly comprehensible that within the National Socialist structure of power, especially in highly political organs like the Counter Espionage, there existed contradictions and cells of resistance which permitted a man like Bonhoeffer to cultivate intensive contacts with foreign countries. It required a convincing personality like that of Bonhoeffer to overcome, by his candour and sincerity, the reserve and mistrust of his important contacts. He also succeeded with Karl Barth, who took the strange German emissary very seriously, because he recognized the essential character of the man and of the information he brought.

I do not remember Bonhoeffer's first visit during the war, in February–March 1941, but I do recall his longer visit in the summer of 1941. He arrived about the time of the German attack on the Soviet Union. The German troops were storming ahead in Russia, with apparently irresistible progress, and our faces grew longer and longer, including that of Visser't Hooft. He was all the more taken aback when Dietrich, on entering his room, by way of greeting him triumphantly exclaimed: 'Now it's nearing the end.' In some bewilderment my Dutch friend asked: 'How? with the Russians?' To which Bonhoeffer, calmly and with absolute conviction, replied: 'No, no, Hitler is nearing an end, through a surfeit of victories.'

From 1942, the diary of my wife gives some information. 14th May, Ascension of Mary: '. . . Bonhoeffer is here again'. 5th July: '. . . I forgot to mention that Bonhoeffer was repeatedly with us, we got on very well with him. We had another evening of discussion with Jacques Courvoisier (professor of church history in Geneva), Henry d'Espine (pastor and professor of practical theology), Professor Lenard, Pasteur Charles Brütsch, Pastor Joh. Schneider, Roland de Pury, Alex. von Weymarn, Frau Visser't Hooft and Pastor Witt, missionary to the Jews in Zürich, who told us of the successful flight from Frankfurt to Zürich of the Jewish-Christian deaconess Elisabeth Neumann.' In the course of these years we saw Bonhoeffer two or three times, in similar informal meetings. In a lively and sober way he told us of Germany, mainly of church affairs, and was keen to hear what we knew and thought.

With the exception of a task of mediation which I carried on for Adam von Trott zu Solz, I did not actively participate in the secret political activities of those years. The reason was that my colleague, Dr. Schönfeld, who was permitted to visit Germany while I was not, kept the contacts open at great personal risk. Bonhoeffer and Schönfeld had little in common, which may be partly explained by the numerous difficulties of co-ordinating the different streams of the German resistance.

As a matter of course I too discussed with Bonhoeffer extensively, and with deep interest, questions concerning Church and politics. But in restrospect I am inclined to think that for him the essential part of our meetings was the friendly companionship where he found relaxation, ease and a much-needed chance to get his breath. Hence the personal note, the anecdote, predominates in my recollections of our meetings in Switzerland.

In helping the refugees my wife had become very experienced in fitting her protégés out, and she knew how to turn her shop-

ping expeditions into little festive occasions. She also took
Dietrich along to her fine Geneva shops to equip him with
shirts and underwear, for his aesthetic feelings clearly suffered
from his worn and shabby clothes. She returned radiantly:
'I have never had such a joyful and grateful customer. Bonhoeffer tried on the new underpants and looked at them bliss-
fully, and only regretted that he could not walk along the street
in them so that people might see their beauty.'

We knew a romantic but rather dingy beer garden situated
above the murmuring waters of the Arve, which had been a
great success with all our guests. But not with Dietrich: the
waitress, the way she served the meal, the importunate animals,
like a cat, a dog, an old duck, a half-naked turkey, begging for
food and pestering the customers – all this offended his sense
of beauty and dignity, and we soon left.

Our most cherished memory is that of his visit at the beginning of September 1941 to our summer-house at Lac
Champex, a small mountain lake in Wallis. He had left the
German anxieties and ghosts entirely behind; he was relaxed
and happy and thoroughly enjoyed the freshness and scents of
early autumn, which is so bright and colourful in the Wallis
mountains. On our long walks he concentrated his joyful
energy on the mushrooms which as an expert he practically
smelt out, and through him we got to know ever new species of
delicious edible mushrooms which we had formerly not risked
picking. In our memories he has remained as we saw him during
that week in the mountains: a great mind, searching for all
that is divine and human, searching the heights and the depths,
never tiring – and equally a great, lovable and simple boy, a
man sheltering in God's mercy.

# The Guest
## OTTO SALOMON

I have only dim memories of my relations with Bonhoeffer from the time when I was working in the Kaiser Verlag, nor can these memories be refreshed, as the letters we exchanged are not extant. In 1930 *Sanctorum Communio* was published, the dissertation of the twenty-one-year-old Bonhoeffer; but the provocative wine-red posters of the National Socialists attracted more attention, even in the Church, than this ecclesiological study of the reality of the empirical Church.

As far as I know, his study *Act and Being*, and *Creation and Fall*, his third publication, were not much read either. Then, in 1937, he sent us the manuscript of his *Cost of Discipleship*. After glancing at it in a cursory fashion I began to be fascinated, devoured it eagerly, and was deeply stirred and excited by it as I had hardly been since reading Barth's *Commentary on Romans*. I reported to my chief and friend Albert Lempp, and after looking at the work himself he was determined to publish it as soon as possible. Now our theological advisers raised objections: the work, they thought, was too 'enthusiastic', it presented a mixture of law and gospel, the *sola fide* principle was abandoned. A small internal strife arose, but Albert Lempp was not diverted from his purpose.

During my time in Munich up to my emigration I only exchanged letters with Dietrich Bonhoeffer but never met him. In 1939 my wife and I settled in our new home above the lake of Zürich. In spring 1941 we heard that Bonhoeffer was looking for a quiet place where he could work. We invited him to stay with us and were happy to have him as our guest, first

# The Guest

in September 1941, and later in May 1942, each time for a week. At our first meeting a point of contact was at once provided by his *Cost of Discipleship*, and also by my little book *The Village on the Hill* which he regarded as an important witness to the inner life of Germany.

For my wife and myself the days spent with Dietrich Bonhoeffer are deeply engraved on our memory. He told us nothing of his activities in the German Resistance, and of his telegrams to the Bishop of Chichester. He slept in our small guest-room and always worked through the night into the early hours of the morning. But in the afternoons we were often together. We were captivated by his charm and by his widely ranging mind. He was so tactful, we hardly noticed that somebody shared our house.

Once when we came home we heard him playing the piano. He at once stopped when he realized that we were back. Several times he invited us out for lunches or dinners and turned these meals into little festive occasions. He loved to eat well. One Sunday he took us to see his friend Erwin Sutz who had been with him, as an exchange student, in the United States. We first attended the service in Rapperswil and then assembled for lunch in the parsonage; for us, this became the basis of a lasting friendship with Pastor Sutz and his wife.

In my study I had intense conversations with Dietrich Bonhoeffer about his writings. I had received *Life Together* immediately after it was published, and I had the impression, from all his publications, that he pursued a straight path in that his interest concentrated on the nature and task of the Church. He agreed with me. In these conversations, he already expressed thoughts which I was to find later in *Letters and Papers from Prison*: his reaching out for a church which was willing and equipped to fulfil her task better as the place where Christ is present in the world. After reading his letters from prison I realized that even then, when he stayed with us, he was turning towards the world and was longing for a church which was open to the world.

One afternoon, after he had fetched his *poste restante* letters, we found him depressed. He said: 'Things are serious for me,' and left the same day.

# Theological Existence
## JACQUES COURVOISIER

The impression we receive in life from our neighbour, and the influence he may exercise upon us, do not depend on the number of our meetings, nor even on the degree of our intimacy with him. There are human beings who leave a deep mark on our existence though we have very rarely met them, whereas others we see more frequently do not leave any remarkable traces on it. In the measure that time passes and year follows year, a selection takes place in our remembrance of those who have crossed our path, a hierarchy falls into shape of those who live on in our memory, and we begin to fathom their contribution to the realization of our own life.

For me Dietrich Bonhoeffer is one of the most striking illustrations of what I have just said. It was not so much what I read of him, but rather his mere presence, his attitude that impressed me most. And if he remains for me an example, and even an authentic witness to him whom he knew how to serve unto death, then this has come about through some of those 'trifles' that grow into meaning, through a spontaneous gesture which suddenly reveals, like lightning, an inner attitude, something that all of a sudden attracts your attention and keeps it under its spell.

I met him twice.

It was during the last war: in 1941 he had come to Geneva and Visser't Hooft, general secretary of the World Council in process of formation, had invited me to meet him one morning at the house the Council first occupied on the Avenue de Champel. This meeting had a twofold interest for me. I had followed the struggle of the Confessing Church with close attention, and now I had the chance to get in touch with one of those who led this struggle in their own country, in the midst of war. Secondly, as I was looking after the spiritual welfare of the prisoners of war and had, in this capacity, sometimes to travel to Germany, I was glad to be able to tell him of my work, hoping, I must confess, that he might be of some help to me from the position he held within the Counter Espionage.

That morning we discussed a lot of things, Visser't Hooft, he and I. We talked about the life of the churches in the world, of the ecumenical reality which was taking shape right across the different events of the time, of the policy the Church was best advised to follow in these circumstances; we also touched upon politics and even strategy, for one just could not ignore that, and Bonhoeffer impressed us as being extremely well informed concerning those problems, which, some people think, have nothing to do with the message of the Church. At the end of our conversation, Bonhoeffer declared that everything we had dealt with was certainly very interesting, but he would prefer to discuss more important and more basic matters. He asked if in the afternoon we might not meet with some theologians in order 'to theologize seriously'. This was done, and in the afternoon we spent several hours at the lake-side with some Geneva pastors and discussed baptism. I do not remember what we said, either in the morning or in the afternoon; but I do remember this man who was involved in the struggle of the Church and in the political struggle at the risk of his life, for whom the essential thing, even under the most threatening circumstances, remained what Karl Barth some years before had called theological existence, and for whom the meaning of political engagement was given in theological engagement.

I saw Dietrich Bonhoeffer a second time in Berlin, in autumn 1942. During my short stay in the German capital we met several times, sometimes alone, sometimes with his brother Klaus. At our conversations there were also present the two brothers John, Eberhard Bethge, a representative of the Red

# Theological Existence

Cross whose name I do not remember, and Herr Delbrück, the brother-in-law of Klaus and Dietrich Bonhoeffer. This is not the place to recount what we talked about. It may be sufficient to indicate that we dealt with the most varied subjects; from my visits to the prison camps where I met with all sorts of difficulties from the side of the authorities, for the overcoming of which Dietrich Bonhoeffer offered me his help, up to questions of German and international politics. What I heard there made me grasp that the game was definitely up for the Germany of the Third Reich, even though the war might linger on for some time.

I still see before me those men who knew with such clarity what awaited their country, and that they might have to seal with their blood the destiny which they had deliberately chosen. They had that calmness and simplicity which at first sight indicates a man who has nothing to fear, either from others or from himself, and whose life runs along smoothly, without remarkable events, in a peaceful country. But this calmness and simplicity created a zone of light and freedom such as I have never experienced before or since. And this is what has remained with me from those conversations.

# Meetings in Early and Late Years

## GERHARD VON RAD

For many years the name and work of Dietrich Bonhoeffer have retained their unabated brilliance; and for those who met him during his lifetime, it is a labour of love to search their memory and call to mind the hours they spent with him. My contribution can only be a very modest one, for I did not share the decisive and sometimes dramatic situations of Dietrich Bonhoeffer's eventful life. And yet I would not have missed our meeting, and the remembrance of his sometimes so unforgettably radiant face.

Like my brother and myself, the Bonhoeffer children spent some of their holidays in their grandmother's house in Tübingen. As both the houses were situated in the lower Neckarhalde, facing one another, and as both grandmothers had of course known each other for years, the grandchildren had a good deal in common. From the years before the First World War I have glorious memories of the riding lessons which brought us boys together. Dietrich was too small to take part in them, we were mostly with his elder brothers Karl-Friedrich and Walter, neither of whom are still alive. Walter was killed in action a few years later. Our families lived, at that time, the broad and comfortable life of the well-to-do, and even the children had a good part in this, though the style they were brought up in was relatively simple for modern ideas. If we wish to understand Dietrich Bonhoeffer, such as his great candour and the worldly assurance which he retained in all situations, we must know that he came from a splendid home, from the family of a Berlin professor which was alive with intellectual stimulus. But we must also realize that it was very rare for a young man of this academic *élite* to decide in favour of the study of theology. The study of theology, and the profession of theologian, were not highly respected in those circles. In a society whose ranks were still clearly discernible, the university theologians stood rather apart, academically and socially.

Only after the First World War did I get to know Dietrich – in Tübingen again, of course. We sometimes made music together. Dietrich was in the sixth form then and played the piano very well. He indulged in playing arpeggios, especially in thumping out the final chords, a habit which he probably soon dropped. Once I took him along to the house of my corporation where I had to read a small theological paper. Only by way of the grandmothers' grapevine did I learn that he liked it. The political questions facing us were more serious. It was the time during and after the Rathenau murders, and a wave of nationalistic resistance against the 'Left' went through the students of Tübingen. The corporations moved, more or less complete, into the barracks for a short spell of military training. I remember vaguely having written Dietrich about it, advising him against joining in.

Much later, when I was a professor in Jena, he suddenly appeared in one of my lectures. I had to expound the fifty-first psalm, and also dwelt on the end of the psalm which had been added later. When we walked home together, we discussed the need for historico-critical research, which I passionately defended against a counter-current which was then arising during the Church struggle. I did not in the least understand my companion, and we quarrelled. Nowadays I would more easily comprehend his concern without giving up mine. But perhaps it was unavoidable that our conversation should run on such narrow lines. When we had lunch with my family the dispute was left aside, though I forget what we talked about then.

Later, during the Second World War, I met him once again, at Ernst Wolf's in Halle. It was one of those rather risky meetings where we discussed what might have to be done 'afterwards'. Neither the Church nor the universities must be unprepared for a possibly sudden end of the National Socialist era. This was the last time I saw him. Through my own fault a meeting with him where we would have been all by ourselves, and which in all likelihood would have been wonderful, did not come about. We had agreed that I should come and see him in Ettal where he stayed for some time. But for some reason I cancelled this. A scrap of his letter on which I noted something down has survived, and I can still read his words: 'I should be glad if this plan materialized.' Even then I must have mistakenly believed that we would have much time left for one another.

# In Discussion with Bonhoeffer
## OSKAR HAMMELSBECK

From 1937 to 1943 I was often with Dietrich Bonhoeffer, but never for more than a day or a few hours, sometimes with other friends, but mostly just the two of us. I think back to those meetings as important and even decisive events in my life. In my memory they merge into a single portrait of extraordinary and undiminished power. It was a moment of almost paralysing stupor, indelibly engraved on my mind, when in May 1945, in the parsonage garden of Reelkirchen-Lippe, Wilhelm Niesel informed me that Dietrich Bonhoeffer and Justus Perels were among the last victims of the National Socialist murders. When I began to recover, I took a consoling and solemn decision to act in future in accordance with Dietrich's will. The isolated occasional meetings I had had with him were now like a bequest, like the engagement of a belated friendship which gives itself to the other as an identity of understanding in faith and in humanity.

When we first met Dietrich was thirty-one and I was thirty-eight. We had looked forward with some anticipation to meeting one another, and when we met there was mutual trust. This led to an exchange, to a readiness to listen to the other, and then again to the silence of thoughtfulness in each other's presence. Every time our happiness increased because each perceived the other's need and openness. To be the friend's guest, often invited, always welcome, helping each other in theology, philosophy, pedagogics, increased our gratefulness for such exceptional, unforeseen blessings at a time when the Church struggle was more and more threatening. That time intensified our happiness and griefs, and it filled with a deeper meaning what we looked for, and found, in such meetings.

# I Knew Dietrich Bonhoeffer

A friendship like ours, which was free from all mannerism and artificiality, reduced to scant and risky visits, challenged in its restraint, and arising from brotherly trust, as between responsible members of the Confessing Church – such friendship has not blossomed after 1945, in our life of restoration and busyness.

To measure the importance of this relationship I must say something about myself. In January 1937 I was dismissed from my post and went to Berlin. I was called there by the second Provisional Church Government, which in the Confessing Church wielded the authority for a church life in accordance with Scripture and Confession, as based on the resolutions adopted by the Dahlem Synod in 1934. Fritz Müller-Dahlem, Martin Albertz, Hans Böhm, Otto Forck and Bernhard Heinrich Fricke formed the Council responsible to Synod and Brethren's Council. After the Breslau Synod in 1936 a Catechists' Seminary was constituted in the Friedenau House of the Gossner Mission. Sixteen to twenty curates – 'illegal' ordinands called the 'young brethren' – had put themselves at the disposal of the Brethren's Councils. They mostly came from the provinces of the Old Prussian Church, and were prepared by the Confessing Church in theological and practical training for their future duties as pastors. Wulf Thiel and I were put in charge of the new seminary. This work was prohibited in autumn 1937, as well as that of the Preachers' Seminaries and the Church colleges, by the so-called 'Himmler Decree'. We continued them camouflaged as 'Team Curacies', until the war made an end of them too.

The directors of all the seminaries of the Confessing Church met now and then, mostly in the Babelsberg parsonage of Pastor Hasse. At the first such meeting, Bonhoeffer and I got acquainted, along with Otto Schmitz, Gerhard Gloege and Hans Joachim Iwand. But the relationship with Dietrich became a special one. Soon we also worked together in other places, such as Magdeburg, dealing with special commissions by the

# In Discussion with Bonhoeffer

Brethren's Council: a memorandum on the Jewish question, on the liquidation of the mentally deficient, on Church discipline. Bonhoeffer brought the drafts, we discussed them and left it to him to compose the final version. I was a novice at this and had to learn all the time, and yet my views were taken quite seriously. Now and then at week-ends we went to see brethren who lived outside Berlin. I remember one such week-end discussion, in Advent 1942, with special clarity; we were with Ernst Wolf in Halle, and also present were Hans Böhm, Gerhard von Rad and Julius Schniewind. On our way there we saw one another at a distance in the crowded corridors of the express train. We could not reach one another and had to clamber through the corridor windows to get on to the platform. There we remained motionless for a moment, as if lifted out of time, in the midst of the crowd pressing past us, for Dietrich had told us that the night before Jochen Klepper had, of his own free will, departed this life with his Jewish wife and stepdaughter, Bibles opened at comforting passages beside them. We had planned to meet Klepper that very Advent.

Being prohibited by the Gestapo to stay in Berlin, Bonhoeffer was confined to his parents' home in Charlottenburg where he was allowed as an 'ex-territorial'. From time to time we sat together in his attic-room. Once only he came along to a secret conference at Hans Lokies' in the Gossner House. Ehrenström from Sweden, Schönfelder from Geneva and Helmut Gollwitzer were also present, to meet the Reverend Mr. Barnes, the personal adviser of F. D. Roosevelt. This took place shortly before the United States entered the war, and our conversation was about the patriotic efforts of the resistance against Hitler.

This meeting confirmed Dietrich and myself in our assessment of the whole situation, and the conclusion we had to draw from it. We looked upon the responsibility of the Church in a way different from some others who after the war were advanced to high State offices which their hidden or open ambitions coveted even then, Church people who were theologically far removed from us, and therefore also remained politically far removed. Dietrich Bonhoeffer had no such political ambition; but he was ready for a responsible deputyship which inexorably pressed itself upon him, as it did upon us, through the special nature of his 'theological' engagement. He would have preferred to do other things. If some of us, urged by the same sense of responsibility, are becoming 'politically' unpopular nowadays, without having any design on political office, then I consider this to be a consequence of carrying out his will. Bracketed together as the communities of Christians and of citizens are, we must warn where warning is necessary, stressing at the same time our approval of the slowly maturing character of a state that our common weal requires.

Bonhoeffer confided to me that he was actively and responsibly involved in the German resistance against Hitler, following his moral conviction that 'the structure of responsible action includes both readiness to accept guilt and freedom' (*Ethics*, p. 209). 'If any man tries to escape guilt in responsibility he detaches himself from the ultimate reality of human existence, and what is more he cuts himself off from the redeeming mystery of Christ's bearing guilt without sin, and he has no share in the divine justification which lies upon this event' (*Ethics*, p. 210). I agreed that he should not tell me the names of the different conspirators, so that if I were to be interviewed by the Gestapo, as more and more of us were at that time, I might be able to answer frankly that I did not know them. There was also the thought of building up a staunch 'reserve', a class of survivors to carry on. How much this was to be needed for the months after the 20th July 1944, we could then only guess.

Bonhoeffer was in touch with different circles of the resistance. There the problem of cultural reconstruction after the expected defeat was discussed, also with regard to schools and the training of teachers in a new republican State. I was asked to compose a memorandum for those circles, of whose members I had only a vague idea. I borrowed somebody else's typewriter, because we had to be cautious. I kept one copy inside a sealed bottle, which I buried in my garden one night. Unfortunately I could not find it when I returned to Berlin for the first time again, in 1947. From his Tegel prison, Dietrich sent me word through Justus Perels that he had heard that the other copies were destroyed; I must not worry that the Gestapo might trace me. Some of the thoughts of that memorandum, though in a more specialized form, have been taken up in the deliberations of the Department for Christian Instruction of the Confessing Church, which met in 1943 behind closed doors to draft a memorandum for the reconstruction of the schools. There were only two copies of this; one has disappeared, the other was smuggled into Switzerland, where it was published in 1945, in the October issue of the *Schweizerisches Evangelisches Schulblatt*. In 1950 I published it in the August issue of *Der Evangelische Erzieher*. This memorandum is the basis of the Church's awareness of its responsibility for the schools, and is part of the tradition of the Confessing Church as expressed in the resolution 'A Word on the Problem of the Schools' (1958).

But we did not only conspire. The essential meaning and fruit of our meeting shows on the one hand Bonhoeffer, theologian 'from his youth', proven by his studies, his early achievements in his dissertation and habilitation, doing work with proletarian youth and students of the technical college, then with congregations in foreign countries and as an exchange student in the United States, as a lecturer at the university of Berlin in undiminished openness for the world, through his experiences in theology and the Church, remaining always close to his highly civilized family, especially in their love of music. And on the other hand the non-theologian, that is the humanist, who had not attended a single lecture on theology, who had read philosophy with Karl Jaspers, history and fine arts with Oncken and Carl Neumann, social studies with Alfred Weber;

who, after a short time of activity in industry, had experienced seven difficult years in adult education among workers and academics, organizing in ever new ventures a voluntary service of unemployed youth; and between being twice dismissed, spending some equally full years in teaching. Different backgrounds, various achievements, but now on a way that was new and common to us both, namely that of the Confessing Church, towards which we both had mingled feelings of criticism, gratitude and amazement. The fatherly friendship which the old Harnack and others extended to Dietrich had, in my life, a parallel in the kind and tolerant welcome given to me by the Heidelberg circle in Marianne Weber's house.

Our first conversations were about our 'experience in catechism'. Dietrich had made two attempts in this direction, one in collaboration with Franz Hildebrandt in 1931 (GS III, 284 ff.), the other, on the dogmatic side, in his work with the ordinands of the Finkenwalde Preachers' Seminary in 1936 (GS III, 335 ff.). Those problems of pedagogics, catechesis and theology claimed our attention again and again. As a consequence Bonhoeffer asked me, when he was in the United States in the summer of 1939, to go for a short time to the Pomeranian forests to look after his group in the Team Curacy along with Bethge and Onnasch.

Dietrich was always keen to hear from me about my preliminary work on Pestalozzi for the seminar on catechetics. Sometimes we tarried over certain notes in a diary, or passages from letters, like the following written by the forty-seven-year-old Pestalozzi in 1793 to his 'spiritual' son, *Staatsrat* Nikolovius: 'I vacillated between feelings which drew me to religion and judgements which led me away from it into the dead path of my own time. The essential element of religion grew cold in my heart, and yet I did not decide against it. . . . The strength of the few isolated religious feelings of my earlier years vanished in the unspeakable misery in which I found myself. I am an agnostic, not because I take impiety for truth, but because the sum of my experiences has in many ways driven the blessing of faith out of my innermost disposition. Thus I am far removed from perfection, and do not know the heights which, so I feel, may be ascended by perfect truth.'

We agreed that only a true Christian, in true temptation, can meditate on unbelief in such a self-critical way and include it in God's reckoning. I recognized the reflection of many such discussions in the posthumous publication of the *Ethics*; in those debates I had been, though not a pupil, yet the one who was mostly learning. This remained our problem: what was God's design with us, as it had been with Pestalozzi, in the various claims of his eternally valid Word? . . .

Another chapter of our life was the interchange of philosophy and theology. In 1942 I was busy with the preparation of a *Festschrift* for Karl Jaspers' sixtieth birthday. Scholars from all over the world, as far as they could still be reached, had contributed forty essays which Gustav Radbruch and I presented on 23rd February 1943. Among the authors were also Bollnow, Dibelius-Heidelberg, W. Flitner, Gadamer, Ernst Hoffmann, van der Leeuw, Thielicke, Sternberger, Alfred Weber, von Wiese and E. Wolf-Freiburg. My contribution was on 'Philosophy as a Theological Problem'. I would not have dared to tackle this theme without my exchange of ideas with Bonhoeffer . . .

What happened, on the occasion of this birthday, as it were in a corner for philosophy and the university, happened in a similar way for us in theology and the Church. Just as the true Church existed (and exists) in a hidden way, cutting across the official Church, and at the same time away from it, so it was with the university. Where the institutions which guaranteed, or should have guaranteed, tradition and continuity, vanished in lies and embarrassment, our immediate effort was to achieve the extraordinary, in venture and suffering. This must not be said presumptuously or with any touch of vanity, but in the piercing awareness that we must and may be pioneers of a free, spiritual, ecumenical colonization in the non-Christian world; in a questioning obedience which is both strict and expectant. This was the spiritual field which Bonhoeffer and I approached from different sides and where we met.

As it became increasingly necessary to be cautious and remain hidden from the Gestapo, we had unfortunately to agree not to exchange letters. Only one brief postcard written by me on 4th February 1943, is extant: 'The quotation from Luther is: "A Christian is a rare bird; would to God most of us were pious heathens who observe natural law – not to mention Christian law."'

This quotation referred to our discussions on natural law. This solitary 'document' is like a tiny signal for a long journey. . . . When the young Bonhoeffer said that he did not wish to become a saint, but to learn to have faith, this, like all spontaneous utterances, has a 'reciprocal' structure. His own life, and the life his Finkenwalde students saw him live, as described in his *Life Together*, down to that 'final signal' from the Tegel prison where he writes about arcane discipline, reveal for us the hidden saint of a modern way of life and faith.

Since Luther took the Protestant way for the Church, turning his back on the monastery, we can no longer venerate saints of the old Church, nor can we follow the path of the saints by practising asceticism. But that does not mean that our Protestant engagement in 'genuine worldliness' proposes any counter-argument. In our conversations the problem of world affirmation cropped up again and again. I brought it with me from my non-churchly 'merely' humanist past, as the nature of my responsibility for the Church which had been kindled by the Barmen theses of 1934; Dietrich's theology, on the other hand, was kindled by this problem. Perhaps we may say in our way what G. K. Chesterton once said of Bernard Shaw, that he has the mark of a true saint, that he is literarily unworldly. Here we have, so it seems to me, the fruitful difference, the opposite pole to both liberalism and orthodoxy. Instead of the bastard offspring of both, personified in the illegitimate consequences of the legitimate attempt at demythologizing and historico-critical research; instead of the theological and practical indifference which is infecting even the life of the congregations, Bonhoeffer's legacy is one of commitment, dialogue and obedience. It is the magic cloak which covers the guilt of unbelief.

The Church for the world – and not the Church for the Church – nor the world for the Church – this irreversible approach to unbelief makes us freebooters of faith and adventurers of the spirit, who, in their firm commitment to the cross and the empty grave of Christ, held by the long lead of Christian faith, plunge into responsibility for the world as missionaries and servants.

This I have learnt from my meeting and friendship with Bonhoeffer: we are to be non-pious in a worldly way and pious in an unworldly way, 'arcane' in the community of saints to which the non-pious of honest godlessness, as for instance in Communism, also belong; we are to be arcane for their sake and for ours. To be worldly in an unworldly way, instead of falling in with the routine of this world; to be pious in a non-pious way, instead of clericalizing the Church which is free in Christ, and the world which in Christ is freed and reconciled; to practise 'non-religious interpretation' of what in biblical language becomes the revelation of Christ's kingdom within the impious world – for us, that is, the Confessing Church, this is his legacy.

This is our witness in the fleeting present and the fleeting world. 'Where the ground bass is firm and clear, there is nothing to stop the counterpoint from being developed to the utmost of its limits' (*Letters and Papers*, p. 131). There is the great people in the East, growing in discipline, estranged from religion; there are great over-populated and undisciplined peoples in Africa and Asia, full of pagan religions, without respect for Christian ways: they are all approaching us, while we remain happily enwrapped in our 'Christian' religions.

Following my suggestion, the town of Wuppertal has called the street where the Teachers' Training College was built, the Dietrich Bonhoeffer Weg. On the first floor a portrait in relief has been hung which was modelled by Dietrich's twin sister Sabine and presented by the Minister of Education for North Rhine-Westphalia; beside it hangs the poem on 'Stations on the Way to Freedom', a present from the Student Christian Movement. They are memorials which urge us not to forget his legacy to pedagogics and the training of teachers. With each new generation of students it grows more difficult to make the spirit of those extraordinary years, the new kind of 'freedom of a Christian man', alive and meaningful. In the desert we are preparing its way, as we must.

# A Meeting in Werder
## WOLF-DIETER ZIMMERMANN

During those years I saw Bonhoeffer only for short times. He was hardly ever in Berlin. In our talks, brief remarks about ethics were followed by longer reflections about affairs in Church and State, about the necessity of resistance and our 'theoretical' task in it. He told me of his travels on behalf of the Counter Espionage, of his meetings with friends in foreign countries. We were all very cautious at that time. Therefore details were omitted, we only talked of the general aspects.

As a result of those sporadic meetings and conversations I only remember details, often rather casual ones, but still typical of that time.

When we met we talked about books. They were part of our life. In them we still found help and happiness. People today can hardly imagine how avidly we read at that time. Books were food in a time of misery. It was difficult to find books that had something to say to us. Once Bonhoeffer recommended to me a Czech history of literature. What had impressed him was that in it literature was not assessed by its truth, its realism, but by its imagination, its dreams. For him, it was a hypothesis worth considering that literature was there to make man dream, to lift him into different worlds. *The Last Puritan* by Santayana was another figure which occupied his mind for some time. He seemed to feel some affinity there. He thought Bultmann's essay on demythologizing far and away one of the most important landmarks in theology. He thought highly of the *Son of Man* by Vilhelm Grönbech (a Danish 'successor' to Kierkegaard), because here the figure of Jesus was freed from the fetters of convention and animated by fresh life.

# I Knew Dietrich Bonhoeffer

Once I met him in Berlin when he was concerned with the ethical problem of marriage and family. We had sometimes disagreed about this problem because as a matter of principle for me, marriage began with being together in the flesh. He always resisted this attitude, saying that that aspect was not decisive. So I was not surprised by his question: 'Is monogamy really a Christian demand?' And he went on to explain that the patriarchs had lived in a different way, and that so many aspects of society and time had to be taken into account. 'In marriage everything is permitted; what else is permitted over and above that?' Here too there was an acceptance of the world come of age, just as it is. The Christian message was not to destroy that adulthood, but to bring salvation and blessing to it.

All these years I have remembered some words of his which seem to be quite typical. He spoke them when we discussed the difficulty of preaching a good sermon. He respected sermons. We were not allowed to criticize sermons that were preached in Finkenwalde. Afterwards, he used to take a stroll with the preacher and tell him, and him alone, what he thought of it. He taught us to accept a preached sermon as a word addressed to us, to which we had to bow. All the same he felt, as we all did, that most sermons were too doctrinaire, too theoretical, too correct. In his opinion, 'there should be a shot of heresy in every good sermon', meaning that it must drop the doctrinaire evenness, must become one-sided, take sides and dare to go beyond the boundaries of what is 'permissible'.

In 1939 I was sent to Werder on the Havel, as an illegal pastor. At the beginning of the war I married. We lived in a small wooden house on a hill which in summer was a meeting-place for many of our friends, in winter very lonely and cold. In November 1942 a few friends joined us at Werder, among them Bonhoeffer. Some had been called up, others expected it any day. Our conversation naturally dwelt on present and future times. Werner von Haeften, an old friend of my family, was now a staff lieutenant of the Army High Command. At the beginning he was rather silent, and we did not ask him about his duties in detail. Suddenly he turned to Bonhoeffer and said: 'Shall I shoot? I can get inside the Führer's headquarters with my revolver. I know where and when the conferences take place. I can get access.' These words frightened us all. They had such an explosive effect that at first each of us endeavoured to calm the others down. The discussion lasted for many hours. Bonhoeffer explained that the shooting by itself meant nothing: something had to be gained by it, a change of circumstances, of the government. The liquidation of Hitler would in itself be no use; things might even become worse. That, he said, made the work of the resistance so difficult, that the 'thereafter' had to be so carefully prepared. Werner von Haeften, who came from an old officers' family, was a gentle type, enthusiastic, idealistic, but also a man of Christian convictions who believed in inherited traditions. He was one of Niemöller's confirmands. Now he suddenly developed enormous energy and was not content with 'theoretical' reflections. He kept asking questions, digging more deeply, he saw his chance and wondered whether he should take it. He reiterated that he might be one of the very few who were able to act, to intervene. He did not consider his life of great importance. Bonhoeffer, on the other hand, exhorted him over and over again to be discreet, to plan clearly and then to see all unforeseen complications through. Nothing should be left to chance. At last von Haeften's questions became direct: 'Shall I . . . ? May I . . . ?' Bonhoeffer answered that he could not decide this for him. The risk had to be taken by him, him alone. If he even spoke of guilt in not making use of a chance, there was certainly as much guilt in light-hearted treatment of the situation. No one could ever emerge without guilt from the situation he was in. But then that guilt was always a guilt borne in suffering.

The two men talked for hours. We others only made some marginal comments. No decision was taken. Werner von Haeften returned to his duties without being given any direction. He had to decide for himself. And later, he did decide. As aide-de-camp to Stauffenberg he was one of those who were involved in the abortive attempt on Hitler's life. He was also one of those who, in the evening of 20th July 1944, were shot in the courtyard of the Army High Command in the Bendlerstrasse. Eye-witnesses tell us that he faced death calmly and bravely.

# An Act of Penitence
## WILLEM A. VISSER'T HOOFT

One of the most difficult decisions in Bonhoeffer's life was whether he should actively join in the resistance against National Socialism and in the preparation for a *coup d'état*. Did Bonhoeffer really have to make this decision? His duties, so he might have told himself, lay in a different field. It was unthinkable, and opposed to the very tradition of his Lutheran theology, that he should take up the fight against authority, and even help in a plot which aimed at abolishing that authority by force. Indeed, almost everything in Bonhoeffer's own life went counter to this. He had always fought for peace. He had been so impressed by Mahatma Gandhi's political methods of powerlessness that he had seriously planned to go to India and stay in Gandhi's Ashram, so that he might learn from him how political conflicts could be solved without force. Moreover, in 1939, when he clearly foresaw that there would be war, he could easily have stayed in the United States where his friends tried everything in their power to keep him. But then he would have denied all he had said about concrete discipleship. So he went back. But first he thought of passive resistance only.

In 1939 I was walking with him up and down the platform of Paddington Station in London. Our discussion centred on the likelihood of his conscription when the Hitler régime started a war, and on whether he should not become a conscientious objector. How did it come about, then, that he took that great decision to be actively involved in preparing the events which had their explosive effect on 20th July 1944? The answer to this question is that here too he could not stop midway. To reject the political system of that time in theory, to reject it by withdrawing into a spiritual realm, was not enough for him. Such an attitude was schizophrenia, it meant that the challenge was not taken seriously, it meant just talk, not action. That in the first instance the Church fought for its own preservation, filled him with sorrow. In a situation where millions of men were threatened in their very existence, it was not a question of saving the Church. But it was mankind that had to be saved. The very conviction which had made him a man of peace, led him into active resistance.

For him, resistance was a salvaging action. There was not only the system of National Socialism which had to be abolished, but also an international order founded on justice had to be established. It was in this spirit that, in September 1941, in Geneva, Bonhoeffer and I worked out a memorandum about the aims to be pursued in peace which a Christian from Holland and one from Germany were both able to advocate. His grasp of political realities was expressed in his view that very much depended on whether a new German Government could count on the immediate support of the Allied powers. But he did not think of a bargain: unlike some continually hesitant generals, he did not wait for the opportune moment when a more favourable strategic or diplomatic position might be achieved. He was concerned with a deeper necessity. The Bishop of Chichester was told that, during a conversation in 1940, Bonhoeffer had said: 'If we claim to be Christians, there is no room for expediency.' And in Sweden in 1942 he added: 'Our action must be understood as an act of penitence.' Similarly he told a small circle of friends in Geneva: 'Only in defeat can we atone for the terrible crimes we have committed against Europe and the world.' Is this fanaticism? Surely not, for it puts into practice the simple biblical truth which is valid for all nations: 'What will it profit a man, if he gains the whole world and forfeits his life?' (Matt. xvi, 26).

Bonhoeffer loved his country. But because of his love, he could not bear to see it become guilty. It was not enough to bewail this fact, to feel sorry about it. A Christian has to try and catch the mad horse, even though it may seem wellnigh impossible or fruitless. There is no fanaticism in this: politically experienced men had reached the same conclusion. But was it not in vain all the same, as the Allies did not take the German resistance movement seriously? I can say from my own experience that when I handed a memorandum of the German resistance to the British Government in 1942, in London, that the Allied governments, both then and in 1944, displayed a very short-sighted attitude. But history has gone on, and today many people all over the world are deeply grateful that there were men who, in times of the greatest terror, proved that there was another Germany. By the total disinterestedness of his action, and by his death, Bonhoeffer anticipated and at the same time strengthened the Stuttgart Confession of Guilt. In this way he contributed decisively to the reconciliation of the nations after the war.

# The Church and the Resistance Movement

## G. K. A. BELL, BISHOP OF CHICHESTER

I am to speak tonight[1] about an episode during the Second World War in which two German pastors and I were deeply involved. I believe it to be of more than ordinary importance. Not only does it show what two brave pastors were prepared to do, at the risk of their lives, in resistance to Hitler, because they were Christians. It also shows that in their view the Christian Church has such a special witness to give that churchmen of one nation have a right to look for help from churchmen of another nation, even though their respective nations are at war. I have accordingly given my lecture the general title of 'The Church and the Resistance Movement'.

The episode took place in Stockholm almost exactly fifteen years ago. My first visit to Stockholm was in 1925, as a delegate of the Church of England to the Universal Christian Conference on Life and Work. And it is to the Stockholm Conference, and to the various meetings of the Universal Christian Council, and my resulting visits to Germany up to the outbreak of war, that I owe my personal relationships with so many German Church leaders. Above all it was through the fellowship of the Council that I gained my first appreciation of the gravity of the crisis with which Germany was faced from 1933 onwards; and that I became a whole-hearted and public supporter of the Confessional Church.

One of the essential marks of this Council was that it sought to find in the common discipleship to Christ a bond of unity transcending all differences of confession, nation and race.

[1] Lecture given in Göttingen on 15th May 1957.

Therefore, when the Second World War broke out, I and other churchmen of different countries who had worked together in this ecumenical fellowship, had a very strong consciousness of the Christian bond. More than this, many German churchmen were well aware of the sympathy felt for the Confessional Church in countries at war with Germany, in the firm stand it continued to make for freedom to preach the Gospel.

In the expression of this Christian fellowship Dr. Hans Schönfeld and Pastor Dietrich Bonhoeffer played remarkable roles. I first knew Hans Schönfeld in 1929, as Secretary for Research of the International Christian Social Institute at Geneva. From the early days of the Nazi régime he had endeavoured to combat the influence of Nazism, and to develop good relations between the German Evangelical Church and church leaders abroad. He lived with his family in Geneva throughout the war, but continued to make journeys to Germany, well knowing the risks he ran.

I first met Dietrich Bonhoeffer in 1933, as German pastor in London, a post he held till 1935. We quickly became intimate friends. He kept me in close touch with the development of the Church struggle, both in London and after his return to Germany. And when he visited England in the spring of 1939 he came to see me in Chichester about two questions in particular. The first as by what means the Confessional Church could be kept in touch with the churches abroad – for 'I am afraid,' he wrote, 'we shall very soon be cut off entirely from our brethren abroad, and that would at any rate mean a tremendous loss to us.' The second was a question personal to himself. 'I am thinking of leaving Germany sometime. The main reason is the compulsory military service to which men of my age (1906) will be called up this year. It seems to me conscientiously impossible to join in a war under present circumstances. On the other hand the Confessional Church as such has not taken any definite attitude in this respect and probably cannot take it as things are. So I should cause a tremendous damage to my brethren if

I were to make a stand on this point which would be regarded by the régime as typical of the hostility of our Church towards the State. . . . Perhaps the worst thing of all is the military oath which I should have to swear.'

We had a prolonged conversation about the whole situation; and I urged him to discuss his tragic dilemma with his own trusted leaders in the Confessing Church. He went to the U.S.A. shortly after. The last contact I had with him before the outbreak of war was in a letter written as he was passing through London at the end of July 1939, on his return from the U.S.A. He had been invited to stay at Union Seminary, New York, as long as he wanted. But (he wrote) 'when news about Danzig reached me, I felt compelled to go back as soon as possible, and to make my decision in Germany' . . . 'It is uncertain,' he added 'when I shall be in this country again.'

The next time I saw Dietrich Bonhoeffer was on 31st May 1942 in Sweden, in the very middle of the war.

My own visit to Sweden came about in this way. Early in 1942 air communications were restored between Britain and Sweden under government auspices, in a limited way. The British Ministry of Information was anxious to use the opportunity to resume contacts between different departments of British and Swedish culture. Sir Kenneth Clark, the Director of the National Gallery, and T. S. Eliot, the poet, were among those who were thus enabled to re-establish connections with art and literature. It was thought desirable to send someone who could renew personal relationships with members of the churches. And as I had many friends in the Church of Sweden, I was invited to undertake this task.

I arrived a little before 3 a.m. on 13th May at the airport of Stockholm, in an aeroplane with a Norwegian pilot and a crew of two, and no other passengers. During the first fortnight I travelled to different parts of Sweden, and met many old friends, and saw many new faces. In the course of my travels I learned far more about what was happening in the world than

# The Church and the Resistance Movement

there was any possibility of learning in Britain. But the first fourteen days, enthralling as they were, did nothing to prepare me for my dramatic encounter with a German pastor, on 26th May, in Stockholm.

I was staying at the time with Mr. Victor Mallet, the British Minister, at the British Legation. That night Nils Ehrenström, a young Swedish pastor, Dr. Hans Schönfeld's assistant in the Research Department at Geneva, took me to the Student Movement House where he introduced me to the Secretary, Mr. Werner. There, to my amazement, I found Dr. Schönfeld himself, fresh from Geneva via Germany. He had come expressly to meet me, the news of my visit having been published in the press. He was clearly suffering under great strain. After warm words of welcome, he spoke first of what he and his colleagues at Geneva were doing. He gave me copies of sermons composed by German Army chaplains for English prisoners of war in Germany, circulated by the office of the German Evangelical Church, of which Dr. Eugen Gerstenmaier was head. He spoke of the work of the YMCA and of the Student Movement. And then, after a while, he reached what was most clearly the object of his visit. He told me about a very important movement inside Germany, in which the Evangelical and the Roman Catholic Churches were playing a leading part. There was, he said, a block of Christians belonging to both confessions who were speaking strongly of three human rights – the right of freedom, the right of the rule of law, and the right to live a Christian life. The movement included trade unionists and working men. These working men challenged him and Dr. Gerstenmaier about the Christian attitude, and asked 'How will your churches face National Socialism'? And he went on to describe a gradual development of Christian groups in military circles, and the civil service, as well as among the trade unionists. There was, he said, a growing movement of opposition to Hitler, and men were on the look-out for a chance to attack him. He spoke of the recent refusal of a number of officers to continue serving in Russia, and how the developments of the previous winter had opened men's eyes – but no lead had been given. And he spoke of a plan for a federation of European nations with a European army under the authority of an executive which might have its headquarters in one of the smaller countries. He added that many Germans were convinced that they must make great sacrifices of their own personal incomes to atone for the damage Germany had done in the occupied territories.

The likelihood of a British victory was not very great, he said, but on the other hand the opposition was aware of impending revolt inside the Nazi Party, of Himmler and his followers against Hitler. The first stage would be the overthrow of Hitler by Himmler and the SS, when the Army would take control of Germany. But – here was Schönfeld's question – would Britain and the United States be willing to make terms with a Germany freed from Hitler? There was no confidence at present that Britain would act differently from the way in which it had acted at Versailles. Although a successful *coup* by Himmler might be of service to the opposition, its members were under no illusion as to the essential preliminary being the elimination of Hitler and Himmler and the Gestapo, and the SS. They also realized that another essential preliminary was the withdrawal of German troops from all occupied territory, with a view to its being taken over by a European authority. But – (they asked) – would the British encourage the leaders of such a revolution to hope for negotiations if the arch-gangsters were removed? The alternative, as he and his friends saw it, was further chaos – with Bolshevism increasing.

I reported the essence of the conversation to the British Minister when I got back to the Legation. He was interested, and told me to go on listening, but not to encourage my visitor; he thought that what Schönfeld said might possibly be a 'peace-feeler'.

Three days later, on the afternoon of 29th May, I saw Schönfeld a second time. Ehrenström and Werner were again

present. There was more discussion about the resistance movement. Schönfeld emphasized the reality of the Church opposition, and quoted General Superintendent Blau in Posen and
Bishop Wurm as particularly striking examples of the leadership,
and also Hanns Lilje. All those opposed to Hitler, he said, were
agreed about the necessity of a Christian basis of life and of
government, and very many were looking to the Church
leaders for help and encouragement. He spoke also of the
significance of the churches' opposition in Norway and Holland.
Our conversation on this occasion lasted about an hour. I asked
Schönfeld to put what he had told me in writing, and he promised to do so.

That evening I went to Upsala to stay with Archbishop
Eidem. I told him of our talks. He had no doubt of Schönfeld's
sincerity, or of the great strain from which he was suffering.
But when we walked together next morning, 30th May, he said
that he thought Schönfeld was too wishful in his thinking, and
found a relief in pouring out to sympathetic ears.

But the next day, Sunday, 31st May, was crucial. I went that
morning to Sigtuna, where I was met by Mr. Harry Johansson,
Director of the Nordic Ecumenical Institute. I lunched with
Dr. Manfred Björquist, head of the Sigtuna Foundation, and
his wife. Then, to my astonishment, after tea, arrived a second
German pastor, Dietrich Bonhoeffer. He had known nothing
of Schönfeld's visit (nor Schönfeld of his). He came with a
courier's pass made out by the Foreign Office in Berlin, through
the help of General Oster, who had planned the whole journey
with Bonhoeffer's brother-in-law, Hans von Dohnanyi, and
Bonhoeffer himself. We told him of the conversations with
Schönfeld, who was not present when Bonhoeffer appeared. I
then suggested that Bonhoeffer and I might talk together in
private, and he and I left the rest and withdrew into another
room.

He gave me messages for his sister in England. He said that
his seminary had been dissolved for the second time, in 1940.

The Gestapo had forbidden him to speak or preach or publish. Nevertheless he had been working hard by day at his book on ethics, and in preparing memoranda for the Brethren's Council, and by night had been engaged in political activity. There had been some danger of his being called up for military service, but he had approached a high officer in the War Office, a friend of the Confessional Church, who had told him 'I will try and keep you out of it'.

Turning then to my conversations with Schönfeld, I emphasized the suspicion with which my report would be met by the British Government when I got home. And I said that, while I understood the immense danger in which he stood, it would undoubtedly be a great help if he were willing to give me any names of leaders in the movement. He agreed readily – although I could see that there was a heavy load on his mind about the whole affair. He named Col.-General Beck, Col.-General von Hammerstein, former chiefs of the General Staff, Herr Goerdeler, former Lord Mayor of Leipzig, Wilhelm Leuschner, former President of the United Trade Unions, Jacob Kaiser, Catholic Trade Union leader. He also mentioned Schacht, as an ambiguous supporter, a 'seismograph of contemporary events'. He emphasized the importance of Beck and Goerdeler. A rising led by them should be taken very seriously. He also said that most of the Field-Marshals and Generals (or those next to them) in the Commands of the Home Front, were reliable – von Kluge, von Bock, Küchler, and though not so likely to come into prominence, von Witzleben.

Our private talk then ended. Schönfeld arrived, and he, Björquist, Johansson, Ehrenström, Bonhoeffer and I joined in general conversation. It was impossible, Schönfeld said, to tell the numbers of those in the opposition. The point was that key positions were held by members of the opposition on the radio, in the big factories, in the water and gas supply stations. There were also close links with the State police. The opposition had been in existence for some time; it was the war which gave it its opportunity, and it had crystallized in the autumn of 1941. If the Allied leaders felt a sense of responsibility for the fate of millions in the occupied countries, they would consider very earnestly the means of preventing great crimes against those peoples. And as to Russia, Schönfeld reminded me that the German Army held 1,000 miles of Russian territory. Stalin could, he considered, be satisfied on the boundary question if the Allies would give a guarantee to the Soviet Government. High German officers, he said, had been impressed with the Soviet *élite*, and believed in the possibility of an understanding.

Here Bonhoeffer broke in. His Christian conscience, he said, was not quite at ease with Schönfeld's ideas. There must be punishment by God. We should not be worthy of such a solution. Our action must be such as the world will understand as an act of repentance. 'Christians do not wish to escape repentance, or chaos, if it is God's will to bring it upon us. We must take this judgement as Christians.' When Bonhoeffer spoke of the importance of the Germans declaring their repentance, I expressed very strong agreement with him. I also spoke of the importance of the Allied armies occupying Berlin. Schönfeld agreed to this, but with the proviso that they occupied Berlin not as conquerors but to assist the German Army against reactionary or hostile forces. The question was asked whether the British would favour the return of a monarchy in Germany. A possible monarch was Prince Louis Ferdinand, who had been brought over from the U.S.A. by Hitler after the death of the Crown Prince's eldest son, and was now living on a farm in East Prussia. He was known to Bonhoeffer, and was a Christian with outspoken social interests.

All this was communicated to me, with a view to my passing it on to the British Government. The resistance movement's aim, I was again told, was the elimination of Hitler, and the setting up of a new *bona fide* German Government which renounced aggression and was based on principles utterly opposed to National Socialism. This new German Government would wish to treat with the Allied Governments for a just peace. But it was urged that it was of little use to incur all the dangers to which the Resistance movement was exposed in fulfilling its aim, if the Allied Governments were going to treat a Germany purged of Hitler and his colleagues in exactly the same way as they proposed to treat a Hitlerite Germany. I was therefore asked to make inquiries, and, if possible, to let the two pastors know the result. It was suggested that should there be any wish on the part of the British Government for preliminary private discussion, Adam von Trott, a friend of Sir Stafford Cripps's son, would be a very suitable person.

I again emphasized the reserve with which my report would be met, and the probability of the Foreign Office taking the view that the whole situation was too uncertain to justify any action on its part. But it was agreed between Bonhoeffer, Schönfeld, Johansson and myself that, if at all possible, the following method of communication should be adopted:

1. If the Foreign Office made no response to my report, I should send a cable to Harry Johansson, Sigtuna, saying simply

*Circumstances too uncertain*

2. If the Foreign Office were sympathetic, but unwilling to commit itself, the message should be

*Friendly reception*

3. If the Foreign Office were willing to authorize some person from the British Legation or the Foreign Office, or a British churchman from London, to discuss possibilities, the message should be

*Paton can come*

(The use of the name *Paton*, a well-known British churchman, did not mean either that this particular person or that a churchman would be chosen, but was simply for convenience.)

It was further agreed that if the Foreign Office proved willing to authorize some person unspecified to discuss possibilities, the following replies, according to circumstances, should be sent either by Johansson from Sigtuna or by Visser't Hooft from

Geneva, naming the kind of representative preferred, and the date before or on which the meeting would take place:

(*a*) If the representative of the Resistance movement wished the person authorized to be a diplomat, a cable would be sent to me at Chichester as follows:

*Please send manuscript before 20th July*

(*b*) If a churchman were preferred to a diplomat at this stage, the cable would say:

*Please send manuscript before 20th July*
*Emphasize religious aspect*

(*c*) If for some reason it was not possible for the representative of the Resistance movement to send anyone to Stockholm, but only to authorize a Swedish third party, who would in fact be Ehrenström, to make further inquiries in London, the cable would say:

*Please arrange to see Strong 20th July*

I should explain that the month to be named in the cable was, for security reasons, to be a month later than the month actually intended – so that 20th July meant in fact 20th June. But it is certainly curious that the date actually agreed on in our conversations as the code date was 20th July – though in a fair copy made later, in order to give more time, it was changed to 30th July. In any case the exact date on which any meeting in Stockholm or London could take place depended on circumstances, which could only be made clear after I had reported to the Foreign Office.

Next day, 1st June, I returned to Stockholm, staying at the British Legation. In the afternoon I saw Johansson, who told me that Björquist refused to allow Sigtuna to be used for purposes of communication between Chichester and the Resistance movement, as inconsistent with Sweden's political neutrality. This meant that messages would have to be sent through Geneva.

I saw Bonhoeffer again the same day, for the last time. He gave me messages for his brother-in-law, Dr. Leibholz, and

# asked me

asked me to tell him that Hans (meaning von Dohnanyi) was active in the good cause. I was also given, I think by Schönfeld, a short written message of greetings from Helmuth von Moltke, simply signed James, for his friend in England, Lionel Curtis of All Souls College, Oxford. In the evening I dined quietly with the British Minister and Mrs. Mallet and had a long talk about the Sigtuna conversations.

The day closed with the receipt of two personal letters, one from Schönfeld enclosing the full text of the statement which I had asked him to prepare, and one from Bonhoeffer. Both pastors spoke of what our meetings had meant, whatever the outcome. 'I cannot express what this fellowship you have shown to us means for us and my fellow Christians who were with us in their thoughts and prayers,' wrote Schönfeld. And Bonhoeffer:

It still seems to me like a dream to have seen you, to have spoken to you, to have heard your voice. I think these days will remain in my memory as some of the greatest of my life. The spirit of fellowship and of Christian brotherliness will carry me through the darkest hours, and even if things go worse than we hope and expect, the light of these few days will never extinguish in my heart. The impressions of these days were so overwhelming that I cannot express them in words.

My visit to Sweden ended officially on 2nd June, but owing to the flying conditions being unfavourable no plane was able to leave until 9th June. I arrived in Scotland on 10th June, and reached home on 11th June.

On 18th June I went to see the head of the Department concerned at the Foreign Office, Mr. Warner, and at his suggestion wrote the same day to Mr. Eden.

Mr. Eden gave me an appointment for 30th June. I gave him a full account of my experiences and conversations. I emphasized my long-standing personal relations with the two pastors, and my association with them, and with Bonhoeffer in particular, before the war, in strong opposition to Hitler and all he stood for. I described the character of the opposition, and the questions put, and gave Mr. Eden all the names which Bonhoeffer had given me. Mr. Eden (my diary notes) was much interested. He appreciated the fact that I had warned the pastors that the British Government was likely to be very reserved in its attitude, as opinion in Britain tended to blame all Germans for tolerating the Nazis for so long. Mr. Eden himself seemed more inclined to think it possible that in some curious way the pastors, without their knowledge, were being used to put out peace feelers. He said that peace feelers had been put out in Turkey and Madrid. He must be scrupulously careful not to enter into even the appearance of negotiations with the enemy, and be able to say truthfully that this was so, both to Russia and to America.

After emphasizing what I believed to be the conviction and reality of the opposition, I handed Mr. Eden the statement which Schönfeld had prepared for me.

The questions put by the opposition (included in an eight-page memorandum of my conversations also given by me to Mr. Eden) may be summarized as follows:

1. If Hitler and his colleagues and the régime were to be eliminated and overthrown by the opposition as above described, would the Allied Governments be willing to treat with a new *bona fide* German Government for a European peace settlement along the lines indicated?

2. While the answer to the first question might be given *privately*, could the Allies announce now *publicly*, in the clearest terms, that if Hitler and the whole régime were overthrown, they would be prepared to negotiate with a new German Government which renounced aggression, for a European peace settlement, along the lines indicated?

I told Mr. Eden that the pastors would be waiting for some sort of reply from me. He promised to consider the whole matter, and write later.

On 13th July I saw Sir Stafford Cripps. He spoke enthusiastically of Adam von Trott: and he told me of his own talk in May with Dr. Visser't Hooft, who had given him a memorandum prepared by von Trott and mentioned in my letter to Mr. Eden. (I heard after the war that Sir Stafford Cripps had shown this memorandum to Mr. Churchill.) Sir Stafford told me that he had informed Visser't Hooft that he might encourage von Trott, *on the basis, however, of Germany being defeated.* When I showed Cripps Schönfeld's statement (which had points of agreement with von Trott's memorandum, but took a more hopeful attitude about co-operation with Russia), it greatly impressed him. He described it as 'far-reaching', and promised to talk it over with Mr. Eden. He agreed that encouragement in any case could do no harm, and at best might do much good.

Four days later, however, Mr. Eden sent me the letter, which was completely negative.

I replied on 25th July, at some length, expressing my disappointment. Mr. Eden wrote again on 4th August. I replied on 17th August 1942.

On 30th July I saw the American Ambassador in London, Mr. J. G. Winant, giving him the same account and leaving the same memorandum and statement with him. I told him that I had seen Mr. Eden. I again emphasized the reality and significance of the opposition in Germany. He received me in a friendly spirit, and listened to what I told him. He also promised to inform the State Department at Washington. But that was all, and I heard no more.

In view of the unwillingness to respond, of which I had indeed warned the two pastors, I could do nothing further by way of communicating with them. The only thing I could do was to send a cable to Visser't Hooft at Geneva, which I did, in these terms, on 23rd July : INTEREST UNDOUBTED, BUT DEEPLY REGRET NO REPLY POSSIBLE. BELL.

The silence of the British Government was a bitter blow to those for whom the pastors stood. By this I mean the main leadership of the Resistance movement. Schönfeld, through Eugen Gerstenmaier, was in special touch with the Kreisau circle, including Helmuth von Moltke and Adam von Trott, while Dietrich Bonhoeffer, through his brother Klaus and his brothers-in-law Hans von Dohnanyi and Rüdiger Schleicher, had links with General Oster and Colonel-General Beck. From Bonhoeffer himself I had a letter dated 28th August. He had heard from his sister, Mrs. Leibholz, of my return home, and hoped that I would write to him. But nothing further passed.

Without divulging anything of my conversations in Sweden, I raised the general question myself in the House of Lords on 10th March 1943, bringing evidence of the reality of an opposition in Germany, and pointing out the necessity of encouragement and assistance if it was to take effective action.[1] But the main burden of the reply given to any later inquiries about Allied support for the Resistance movement in Germany was that the cleansing of Germany was a German duty, to be performed for its own sake, and that no promises in advance could be expected from the Allies.

Then, on 20th July 1944, as all the world knows, the Plot took effect, and failed. The men named to me just over two years before by Bonhoeffer were among the chief conspirators who, in Hitler's words, were 'exterminated mercilessly'. Bonhoeffer had been already arrested by the Gestapo on 5th April 1943, and was in prison when the attempt was made. On 9th April 1945, together with Admiral Canaris and General Oster, he was executed in the concentration camp at Flossenbürg, aged thirty-nine. When he was taken off to the scaffold on 8th April he sent me a message through Captain Payne Best, a British fellow prisoner:

Tell him [he said] that for me this is the end but also the beginning – with him I believe in the principle of our Universal Christian brotherhood which rises above all

[1] *The Church and Humanity 1939–1946* by G. K. A. Bell, Longmans, Green & Co., London, pp. 95–109.

national interests, and that our victory is certain – tell him too that I have never forgotten his words at our last meeting.

In the same month other members of the Bonhoeffer family met a similar fate. Dietrich's brother, Klaus, and his two brothers-in-law, Hans von Dohnanyi and Rüdiger Schleicher, were all murdered.

Hans Schönfeld's sufferings were of a different kind, but they were very deep. He endured great strain, and faced the many dangers to which he was exposed during his journeys from Germany to Geneva with high courage. His health after the war deteriorated greatly, and he fell a victim to a prolonged nervous illness. He died in Frankfurt-am-Main on 1st September 1954 at the age of fifty-four.

I know that it is said by some leading British historians and others that the Plot of 20th July was doomed to failure, that the Resistance was vacillating, rash and disunited, and that the German generals would never have brought themselves to take decisive action. I know too that in the summer of 1942 the position of the Allies was critical from the military point of view, and that those charged with the direction of the war were absorbed in dealing with military problems. Nevertheless my own strong conviction is that the negative attitude of the Allies was wrong; that the sound and statesmanlike policy would have been to offer a positive response to the approaches made at such terrible risk; and that the failure to do so was tragic. But the principal point which I want to urge is this. The driving force behind the Resistance movement was a moral force. I do not dispute that there were different elements in it, not all on the same level of moral and religious inspiration. But its leaders were men of high ideals, to whom Hitler and all his works were an abomination. Its finest spirits stood for a Germany purged of totalitarianism and the lust for aggression. It was of the very essence of the Resistance movement that it should aim at the building up of the national, economic and social life, both of

# The Church and the Resistance Movement

Germany and Europe, on the fundamental principles of the Christian faith and life. It is no wonder, surely, that members of the Christian Church in Germany, both Protestants and Catholics, should be prominent in it. Nor should it be surprising that churchmen outside Germany who knew something of the conflict within that country, should give it public support, even in time of war. I count it personally a high honour to have been with these two German pastors who came to Sweden in 1942 in the cause of truth, justice and freedom. In the words of Dietrich Bonhoeffer, 'I believe in the principle of our Universal Christian brotherhood which rises above all national interest': Finally I make bold to claim that, at this juncture in human history, the future of Europe and of the whole world of nations depends on whether or not statesmen and leaders in the different walks of life show the same brave and disinterested loyalty to truth, justice and freedom, in national and international affairs, that the finest spirits of the Resistance movement in Germany showed during the Second World War.

# VI

# Meetings in Tegel

## SUSANNE DRESS

At the gate I receive my number and permit. Broad lanes between red walls, barred windows behind fenced-in court-yards. I am pushing my bicycle – perhaps we are not allowed to ride it here. The air in the waiting-room is even thicker than in the corridors, but for weeks I have known that 'In default of permission to see prisoner make straight for parcels office'. The waiting people are glued to the narrow wooden bench along the wall, holding their small suitcases and parcels carefully, almost tenderly, in their laps. Nobody here who has not put on a mask; no word is said beyond what is necessary. So we sit and wait, rigid, a silent community.

My turn has come to hand in what I have brought for Dietrich. Strict examination. Nobody ever notices the dots under the letters in the books which we bring and fetch, our code. A new period of waiting till I am called again. Here are the things that have just passed through Dietrich's hands, books, used underwear, empty waterproof cartons which he has carefully preserved; they are precious, for it is prohibited to bring food in glass jars and tins. Again everything is examined. There is a piece of paper on which Dietrich has written, in a slightly unfamiliar very clear handwriting, for the benefit of the control I suppose; he is asking for handkerchiefs, certain books, soap or other small items which are permitted. No greeting, no signature. I am allowed to read it, to copy it. He will have to wait for them for a week.

I am just packing everything into my shabby little suitcase when one of the uniformed men beckons to me saying: 'You wanted to make a telephone call.' Later I hear that this is Sergeant Holzendorf. Of course, why shouldn't I? He may want to give me a message. I walk behind him, through narrow greyish corridors. Not a word. Then he opens a door, says 'fifteen minutes', steps back, and closes the door behind me. I see my brother before me.

How good that we have been taught by our parents to control even our most violent emotions. Still, we remain silent while we press one another's hand. Then I automatically cover the telephone on the desk with my jacket and explain why I am here: 'I have to make a call.' 'I did not know why I was asked to come here,' Dietrich says, 'how terribly nice of Holzendorf.' And with that adjective so often used by him in past times, our childhood and youth is back with us and the horror of those closed walls has gone. If the sergeant in charge in the detention prison of Tegel can be 'terribly nice', then this is an unbroken Dietrich who has retained his old well-intentioned way of accepting and appreciating people.

Now question follows question about the family, especially our imprisoned brother-in-law Hans von Dohnanyi, and my answers follow with that same rapidity which is so natural to us brothers and sisters but makes listeners, even friends, slightly dizzy. How long may a telephone conversation in a prison take without rousing suspicion? Anyway, what a blessing, for the few minutes granted to us, that we have been trained at home to say only what is essential, and to say it briefly, however reserved this laconic way of speech as well as the control of our feelings may seem.

Most important is some news for our brother-in-law. This is a result of the interrogations and may be secretly forwarded to him. Dietrich wants our views about the situation. If we did not know that our wishes are fathers to our thoughts, we should be better able to estimate the situation clearly. As it is, we find a common ground, my opinion arising out of the opposition of the middle class and the work of the Church, his from life in the military detention prison: it cannot last much longer, the whole structure is coming apart, on the economic, the military, the human level. Dietrich smiles: 'It cannot last much longer, just wait a little while.' Then he asks about his godson, my little Michael. When he visited us the last time, the six-year-old boy impressed him by singing all the stanzas of the hymn, 'Why should I grieve', by heart in his bed at night. We had not been so sure about the second stanza, Dietrich and I, but the little boy, noticing it, recited it to us with a loud voice: 'Naked I lay on the floor when I came, when I drew my first breath; naked I shall depart again when I shall flee from the earth, a shadow.' 'I have learnt all the stanzas now by heart,' Dietrich says. I remember the evening so well, and the child's voice in the dark. It concerned us, but thank God, we had no premonition to what extent. It is an effort for us now not to weaken, for soon our time will have run out. A few short messages, some requests: 'Do tell us what you need and should like, we certainly won't miss it, and many friends want to help.' Slowly the door is opening, I throw my jacket over my shoulders. Dietrich keeps in the background in case Holzendorf is not alone. But he is alone. 'May God protect you during the raids.' 'You too, all of you here.' The genuinely good, brave and I may even say noble Holzendorf, who tried to lighten the burden of prison life for others too, is later to be the victim of an air raid. But only later; another two times I am allowed to phone when I arrive with my suitcase in Tegel and find Dietrich in Holzendorf's room. Of course this must only happen at long intervals, so that we may not rouse any suspicion.

But Holzendorf has still another way of helping us. While I am packing the returned things into my suitcase, I hear somebody calling: 'Bonhoeffer to go downstairs for exercise.' There is the large prison yard and if I dawdle I shall just manage to pass it when Dietrich emerges with his guard. Thus we at least see one another, give the other a slight nod, and try to put all the assurance, which we so painfully preserve, into our eyes, our gestures, our thoughts.

While we are talking together once again during my

'telephone call', Dietrich says: 'Why not apply for permission to talk to me?' I have never done it because I did not want to deprive my parents and his fiancée of the few possibilities. But now I make an application. A few weeks later I am sitting with my visitor's permit in the evil-smelling waiting-room. After a little while I am called out and taken to the private office of the prison commandant. He is extremely polite, practically ceremoniously courteous. I find this embarrassing and quite out of place. Perhaps he is suffering from the awkwardness of the situation too, for after all my mother's cousin as City Commandant of Berlin is his chief. He assures me that my brother's health is excellent, after a small 'indisposition', and that he will be 'brought' any moment. This 'being brought' seems to me the very proof of his 'indisposition', but of course I am politely silent. Anyway I do not know how to address the gentleman. I have an inhibition about learning all about military ranks and uniforms which is not quite involuntary. Now Dietrich is sitting beside me, both of us in armchairs, the commandant opposite, behind his desk; Dietrich addresses him as 'Herr Hauptmann', and we exchange trivialities. The few minutes in the sergeant's room give us a much livelier feeling of nearness and reality than this official conversation. But we are happy to be together. Everything becomes immensely important, Dietrich's voice, his appearance, the way he asks questions, everything serves to make me see how he lives, how he deals with the situation; whether he suffers more than he admits, or is as strong and capable of suffering as he always seemed to me to be. Now and then our overseer intervenes in the conversation by remarking for instance how stimulating it is to take a walk with Dietrich. He means to imply that in view of Dietrich's powerful relations he himself goes to the trouble of giving Bonhoeffer the prescribed exercise. There are the usual inquiries about family, friends; there are repeated expressions of astonishment, meant for the listener, about the long time of imprisonment, since we have not the faintest notion of the crime he is charged with. There are a few remarks about the books I brought him, and a few careful questions about Church affairs which again are answered for the benefit of the listener. I tell him of the amusing behaviour of my boys during the last search of our house by the Gestapo, and Dietrich wants to know more about it. After all, our Herr Hauptmann has to hear something about the life of ordinary citizens. It makes him a little restless, but there is a knock. Dietrich is being taken away. I am asked to stay for a moment, my visitor's permit is stamped and then I am dismissed in perfect style with the assurance that as far as he is concerned, Dietrich's well-being is in the best of hands. The following night there is another air raid on Berlin.

In the hope of seeing his uncle, my little Michael wants to come with me to Tegel. I promise it for a day 'when there has been no air raid in the night and the district railway is working'. So one day we are sitting together on the narrow wooden bench and he stares hopefully at the uniformed men, waiting for one of them to speak the 'Open sesame', for the heavy doors and iron bars and the clanging bunches of keys are as in a fairy-tale. But his wish is not fulfilled, and we must go home. On our way to the outer gate I can only show him the windows behind one of which Uncle Dietrich now lives. One of Dietrich's letters later indicates that he has heard of the visit of his little nephew.

Friday, 28th July 1944. This time the way from Dahlem to Tegel on my bicycle is very, very long. I stop at our parents' home at Station Heerstrasse to gather the latest news, and things for Dietrich. Will the situation have changed for him, as the nephew of the City Commandant von Hase who has just been hanged? Will he still be permitted to receive his laundry, food and cigarettes? Shall I be able to report about him to my parents? Our friend Holzendorf has been dead since January. But Dietrich has now and then managed to take his half-hour's walk in the courtyard on Fridays just after receiving his things. Nowadays he is no longer accompanied by the captain but by a simple guard; but the man seems to be a friend and in the know.

I am admitted, hand in our gifts, they are examined, I have to wait – Dietrich's returns are examined, handed out to me – everything is as usual. Now I have to pack everything very slowly in case he is coming down for exercise. I unlock my bicycle in a very laborious way, gazing anxiously at the prison yard. Nothing. I struggle to tie up my suitcase, begin to push my bike, with a last look through the fence, to the corner of the yard where he always comes from. And there he is walking calmly down the broad way towards me, with his guard. Fortunately I have learned, as the youngest of eight brothers and sisters, to wangle my way through when I wanted to get something. I have to speak to Dietrich now without attracting attention. In a second both valves have been screwed off, I lean the bike against the wall and, with my back turned to the two men, I am busy with the pump. Now they stop behind me. It has worked! 'Flat tyres? Can I help you?' the guard asks in a loud voice, and Dietrich whispers: 'We can talk, Herr Knobloch is absolutely safe.' I thank the man ostentatiously, hand him my pump and the valves, bend over the bicycle showing interest, while our good spirit and helper squats down beside it, eagerly fumbling with it. Dietrich is standing quite near, unconcerned, and speaks without moving his lips. My answers across the bicycle, in a subdued voice, must seem harmless, as if I was giving advice about the tyres. 'No, our brother Klaus is free, but [Dietrich's friend] Hans von Haeften and his wife have been arrested. Last Sunday he was with us in the Dahlem church for communion. After the service, he spoke with us, very calmly, about his probable near end. His brother was Stauffenberg's aide-de-camp. In the evening we waited in vain for his promised visit.' Dietrich is very perturbed, his friend leaves five small children behind. Our brother-in-law Hans [von Dohnanyi] is still lying paralysed in prison after a severe attack of diphtheria. That is a comforting thought in the present situation. Dietrich is already informed about the death of our uncle, about anything announced on the radio, even on the BBC. He hears it in the sick quarters. He is perturbed that the West has taken so little notice of the whole matter of the rising against Hitler. For himself, the conditions of prison life have not become harsher. But he looks so ill, worse than ever before. 'Things may take a turn different from what we hoped, after all.' And yet the hopeful, wishful thinking: perhaps now they will all realize what is going on, perhaps the end will come soon, the restlessness is growing, too many have been hit. 'There has never been so much going on with knocking signs at night as these days,' he says. Herr Knobloch has taken almost an hour to replace the two valves and blow up the tyres. In a harmless way, I thank the two gentlemen with a hearty hand-shake and push my bike to the gate without looking round, for now my tears are falling; but the warders are accustomed to seeing that.

I hardly notice how I get home, I am so happy to be able to tell our parents that I have seen and spoken with Dietrich. 'Knocking signs at night,' I think, 'it began with knocking signs.' One day when we three 'little ones' no longer slept together, he told me and my sister Sabine: 'During the day we think far too little of God, and in the evening after prayer I immediately think of other things and hear how you two next door start chattering. Shall I, every time God comes into my mind at night, knock three times at your wall so that you will think of him too?' Three knocks – sometimes I still hear them. I wonder whether Dietrich remembered them in his cell. On 28th July 1944 I met my brother Dietrich for the last time.

# The Freedom of the Prisoner

## HARALD POELCHAU

I first met Dietrich Bonhoeffer in prison. At the beginning he was put in solitary confinement. Often when I was on night duty I passed his cell, which bore a notice prohibiting all access. I tried to get in touch with him when, in the quiet hours of the night, nobody was around; but in this house of cells where you heard every sound, I did not dare to flout the order and unlock his door. His neighbour in the next cell would have reported it the next morning. So I had to wait.

Soon, however, he was transferred to the third storey, to a cell looking south with a sweeping view across the prison yard to the pine forest. For many months I was able to visit him almost daily. Towards his fellow-prisoners and warders he was as he himself describes it in his poem, 'Who Am I?': 'Calmly, cheerfully, firmly, like a squire in his country-house. Who Am I? They often tell me that I speak to my warders freely and friendly and clearly, as though it were mine to command.' During the day he worked hard on the many books he had (Stifter, Gotthelf, Weizsäcker), and on drafts of his own, some of which have survived, such as an exposition of the first three commandments. His work was frequently interrupted by air-raid warnings and attacks, during one of which his wing was hit by a bomb which crashed through two storeys and killed the prisoners in their cells. During the air raids, and during the exercises in the prison yard, Bonhoeffer became the pastor of his fellow prisoners, and even, increasingly, of his warders. The medical orderlies especially became attached to him, and often sat up late talking with him in the sick quarters.

Towards the end of June 1944 he moved so freely about the house that we seriously wondered whether he should not escape, which could have been easily arranged. He did not want to do it; it would have meant inflicting himself on somebody who had to hide him. Also, he felt comparatively safe in Tegel as long as his uncle, General von Hase, was City Commandant of Berlin. Once his uncle came to see him in prison, stayed for five hours, drank champagne with him and thus raised Bonhoeffer's position officially – a position which he had already secured in the hearts of men through his very personality. But now the situation was almost grotesque. Bonhoeffer writes about it: 'It is incredibly comical to see how everybody runs around flapping his wings and, apart from some notable exceptions, outdoes the others in lack of dignity.' This happened on 30th June 1944. Five weeks later von Hase was executed. Bonhoeffer's connection with the outside world was kept open by Justus Perels who regularly visited him without regard for the danger that threatened himself. His calm and reliable advice was a great comfort to Bonhoeffer. Perels was arrested on 5th October and shot in the night of the 22nd and 23rd April 1945. When I visited Bonhoeffer, our conversations were not entirely of a pastoral kind, though this was central. There was give and take, and I owe much to that year with him. Often he was the pastor and I the prisoner. But there were times of great cheerfulness too. One day he asked me to have a cup of coffee with him, the way you might invite somebody in the desert. When I stared at him in astonishment he told me of his neighbour in the next door cell, an English officer, who had invited both of us if I could risk locking him in the other cell. We slipped across at a propitious moment, and had a little party, with a primus stove propped up in the heap of sand which was in a corner of each cell for use during air raids. We had coffee, white bread which had been saved for the occasion, and we had talk, both serious and gay, which helped us to forget the war.

But Bonhoeffer's situation could hardly be called idyllic. He had to struggle with many anxieties, not so much concerning his personal fate as that of his own people, who had incurred such guilt through the wrongs done to Jews and foreigners. For the sake of his people he had tried, but unsuccessfully, to initiate discussions with Britain via Sweden; and as a result he was arrested. We never talked much about what was to come, and were not aware of the danger in which Bonhoeffer stood. But when we heard of the 20th July and of the arrest of von Hase and all his friends, he was aware of how great the catastrophe was. His letter of 21st July shows it clearly, brief and reserved though it is. In October he was transferred from Tegel to the Gestapo prison in the Prinz-Albrecht-Strasse; the regular visits from his parents and his fiancée stopped, and contact with the outside world became very meagre.

His Christian faith, and his gift for meeting every kind of person in the right spirit, distinguished Dietrich Bonhoeffer from the mass of his fellow-prisoners; all the same, he felt one with them. At Christmas 1943 I asked him to help me draft a sheet which could be handed in to all the cells, including those of the criminals. He joyfully set to work on this, beside all his scholarly studies. It was in this way that his prayers for his fellow-prisoners were written, which are inspired by such a deep feeling of brotherliness that they speak to all times, for the thoughtful person as well as for the simple seeker. They are the expression of his faith, and the reports of his fellow-sufferers from the days when direct communication was no longer possible, tell us that he retained this inner faith to the hour of his death.

O God,
Early in the morning do I cry unto thee.
Help me to pray,
And to think only of thee.
I cannot pray alone.

In me there is darkness,
But with thee there is light.
I am lonely, but thou leavest me not.

## The Freedom of the Prisoner

I am feeble in heart, but thou leavest me not.
I am restless, but with thee there is peace.
In me there is bitterness, but with thee there is patience;
Thy ways are past understanding, but
Thou knowest the way for me.

# In Prison with Dietrich Bonhoeffer

## FABIAN VON SCHLABRENDORFF

After the 20th July 1944 the interrogation prisons of the Gestapo in Germany were filled with people who were accused of having participated in, or known about, the *coup d'état* and the attempt on Hitler's life. It was especially to the prison in the building of the Gestapo Headquarters in the Prinz-Albrecht-Strasse in Berlin that people were delivered up every day; from there they were taken for trial to the People's Court and, after being sentenced to death, handed over to the places of execution. Surely never since the days when the Christians were persecuted in ancient Rome did such an abundance of noble, truly Christian men and women populate the prisons and dungeons of such barbarians as the SS and the Gestapo. Among those who suffered the fearful fate of being arrested in the Third Reich, even before the 20th July 1944, was Dietrich Bonhoeffer, and people more qualified than I can witness to his human and spiritual gifts and his rank as a Protestant theologian. Before the 20th July 1944 his fate seemed bearable, and offered some hope for his future; but this vanished when the bomb thrown in Hitler's headquarters killed some of his entourage, but not the tyrant himself. The countless meetings and discussions which prepared the *coup d'état* of the 20th July could be successfully kept dark; but its failure automatically brought about the discovery and liquidation of all those who had started, and carried on for years, the struggle against Hitler. So on 8th October 1944 Dietrich Bonhoeffer was taken from the military prison in Tegel to the prison in the Gestapo Headquarters. There I saw him for the first time at night when during an air raid we prisoners were taken from our cells to a cement shelter in the prison yard. This was not done from humane considerations, to protect our lives, but the Gestapo feared we might be killed by a bomb before they had forced the information out of us which they hoped to get.

I must admit I was filled with alarm when I caught sight of Dietrich Bonhoeffer. But when I saw his upright figure and his imperturbable glance, I took comfort, and I knew that he had recognized me without losing his composure. First he was in cell 19. The very next morning I was able to have a word with him in the wash-room which had facilities for several people, though the rule was that the prisoners were not allowed to speak to one another, and this was normally strictly watched. We had known each other for some time before the war began, and our relationship had become even closer through Dietrich Bonhoeffer's engagement to my cousin Maria von Wedemeyer. Dietrich let me know immediately that he was determined to resist all the efforts of the Gestapo, and to reveal nothing of what our friends' fates made it our duty to keep dark. A few days later he was transferred from cell 19 to cell 24. This made him my neighbour, and gave us the chance to communicate with one another and have short conversations every day. In the mornings we hurried together into a niche of the wash-room where we could have a shower, and we eagerly indulged in this opportunity, though the water was cold, for in this way we could escape the supervision of our warders and have a brief exchange of thoughts. In the evenings this was repeated, and the doors of our cells remained open until all the prisoners of our corridor had returned. During that time we were eagerly talking to one another through the slits in the hinges of the door separating us. Finally, we saw one another during the air-raid warnings which happened every day and night, and where we seized every opportunity to inform each other of our thoughts and experiences. Only someone who has been in strict solitary confinement for a long period of time is able to understand what this chance of talking to somebody meant for us during those long months. Dietrich Bonhoeffer told me of his interrogations:

how the very first time they had threatened to apply tor-
ture, and with what brutality the proceedings were carried
through. He characterized his interrogations with one short
word: disgusting. His noble and pure soul must have suffered
deeply. But he betrayed no sign of it. He was always good-
tempered, always of the same kindliness and politeness towards
everybody, so that to my surprise, within a short time, he had
won over his warders, who were not always kindly disposed.
It was significant for our relationship that he was rather the
hopeful one while I now and then suffered from depressions.
He always cheered me up and comforted me, he never tired of
repeating that the only fight which is lost is that which we give
up. Many little notes he slipped into my hands on which he
had written biblical words of comfort and hope. He looked with
optimism at his own situation too. He repeatedly told me the
Gestapo had no clue to his real activities. He had been able to
trivialize his acquaintance with Goerdeler. His connection with
Perels, the justiciary of the Confessing Church, was not of
sufficient importance to serve as an indictment. And as for his
foreign travels and meetings with English Church dignitaries,
the Gestapo did not grasp their purpose and point. If the in-
vestigations were to carry on at the present pace, years might
pass till they reached their conclusions. He was full of hope,
he even conjectured that he might be set free without a trial,
if some influential person had the courage to intercede on his
behalf with the Gestapo. He also thought he had represented
his relation to his brother-in-law, *Reichsgerichtsrat* von Dohnanyi,
in a plausible way to his interlocutors, so that this was not a
heavy charge against him. When Dohnanyi was also delivered
to the Prinz-Albrecht-Strasse prison, Dietrich even managed to
get in touch with him. When we returned after an air-raid
warning from our cement shelter, his brother-in-law lay on a
stretcher in his cell, paralysed in both legs. With an alacrity that
nobody would have believed him capable of, Dietrich Bonhoeffer
suddenly dived into the open cell of his brother-in-law. It

seemed a miracle that none of the warders saw it. But Dietrich also succeeded in the more difficult part of his venture, in emerging from Dohnanyi's cell unnoticed and getting into line with the column of prisoners who were filing along the corridor. That same evening he told me that he had agreed with Dohnanyi upon all essential points of their further testimony. Only once he thought things had taken a turn for the worse, for he had been threatened with the arrest of his fiancée, his aged parents and his sisters unless his statements were more comprehensive. Then he judged the time had come frankly to declare that he was an enemy of National Socialism. His attitude, so he had stated, was rooted in his Christian convictions. In his talks with me he stuck to his opinion that no evidence could be produced which justified a prosecution for high treason.

As neighbours in our prison cells we also shared joy and sorrow in our personal and human life. The few things which we possessed and which we were allowed to accept from our relations and friends we exchanged according to our needs. With shining eyes he told me of the letters from his fiancée and his parents whose love he felt near him even in the Gestapo prison. Each Wednesday he received his laundry parcel which also contained cigars, apples or bread, and he never omitted to share them with me the same evening when we were not watched; it delighted him that even in prison you were able to help your neighbour, and let him share in what you had.

On the morning of 3rd February 1945 an air raid turned the city of Berlin into a heap of rubble; the buildings of the Gestapo Headquarters were also burnt out. Tightly squeezed together we were standing in our air-raid shelter when a bomb hit it with an enormous explosion. For a second it seemed as if the shelter were bursting and the ceiling crashing down on top of us. It rocked like a ship tossing in the storm, but it held. At that moment Dietrich Bonhoeffer showed his mettle. He remained quite calm, he did not move a muscle, but stood motionless and relaxed as if nothing had happened.

On 7th February 1945 in the morning I spoke to him for the last time. On the same day around noon the number of his cell was called up amongst others. The prisoners were divided into two groups. Bonhoeffer's was transported to Buchenwald, the concentration camp near Weimar. From there he was taken to Regensburg on 3rd April 1945 and on 5th April to Schönberg, another concentration camp. I got this undoubtedly reliable information later from my fellow-prisoners when I questioned them about it. At that time when the Nazi rule was in a state of collapse and the prisons so crowded that it was no longer possible to keep the prisoners apart, Dietrich Bonhoeffer again acted as the appointed servant to the Word of Jesus Christ. He held devotional meetings, comforted those in despair, tried to raise their courage, and in his imperturbability was an example for many.

Meantime I had also been taken from Berlin to the concentration camp of Flossenbürg, which was known as an extermination camp. In the night of the 7th and 8th April 1945 I was wakened and asked my name. A few minutes later I was wakened again. The warder upbraided me for giving him a wrong name, I was Bonhoeffer. When I denied it he left me again. On 10th April 1945 a slightly tipsy warder of the SS told me that they had had to hang people of the *Abwehr* yesterday. Those warders who had helped with it had received an additional ration of schnapps and blood-sausage. The execution had not taken place as the consequence of a judicial verdict, but Himmler on his own authority had ordered the liquidation by hanging. When I asked who had been hanged, the warder named Admiral Canaris, General Oster and Bonhoeffer. I learnt much later from a fellow-prisoner and an SS warder that on 8th April Bonhoeffer had been taken from Schönberg to Flossenbürg. There in the course of the 9th April 1945 his few belongings had been deposited in the guard-room, among them a Bible and a volume of Goethe both of which bore Dietrich Bonhoeffer's name. Thus no doubt remains that Dietrich Bonhoeffer was hanged by the SS in the Flossenbürg concentration camp on 9th April 1945, at 6 a.m. Only those who knew him understand the loss which his family, his fiancée and his friends have had to lament. His death robbed not only Germany but the whole of Christendom of a pioneer of Christianity who excelled in every gift of mind and soul.

When after several months I returned to my home, which had been destroyed by bombs, I at first saw nothing but rubble. Anything which the bombs had spared had been stolen. Only one book lay undamaged among the bricks and mortar: Dietrich Bonhoeffer's *Cost of Discipleship*.

# A Report from Flossenbürg
## H. FISCHER-HÜLLSTRUNG

On the morning of that day between five and six o'clock the prisoners, among them Admiral Canaris, General Oster, General Thomas and *Reichgerichtsrat* Sack were taken from their cells, and the verdicts of the court martial read out to them. Through the half-open door in one room of the huts I saw Pastor Bonhoeffer, before taking off his prison garb, kneeling on the floor praying fervently to his God. I was most deeply moved by the way this lovable man prayed, so devout and so certain that God heard his prayer. At the place of execution, he again said a short prayer and then climbed the steps to the gallows, brave and composed. His death ensued after a few seconds. In the almost fifty years that I worked as a doctor, I have hardly ever seen a man die so entirely submissive to the will of God.

# The Contributors

GEORGE BELL, The Rt. Rev., DD, 1883–1958; educated at Westminster School, Christ Church Oxford, Wells Theological College; Dean of Canterbury 1924–9; Bishop of Chichester 1929–58; Chairman of the Universal Christian Council for Life and Work 1934–6; Chairman of the Church of England Committee for Non-Aryan Christians 1937; Vice-Chairman of the Christian Council for Refugees 1938; Chairman of the Famine Relief Committee 1942–5; Chairman of the Church of England Council on Foreign Relations 1945; Chairman of the Central Committee of the World Council of Churches 1948–54; Hon. President of the World Council of Churches 1954.

EBERHARD BETHGE, Pastor, DD, born 1909 in Warchau near Magdeburg, Bonhoeffer's collaborator in Finkenwalde and in the Team Curacy. After many years of ministry in the German Speaking Congregation in London has become the director of the Pastoral College of the Rhenish Church in Rengsdorf. His contribution to this book is an extract from his Bonhoeffer biography to be published shortly.

EMMI BONHOEFFER, born in 1905 in Berlin, daughter of the historian Hans Delbrück and widow of Dietrich Bonhoeffer's elder brother, the lawyer Klaus Bonhoeffer, murdered by the Gestapo in 1940. She lives in Frankfurt and works for various charitable institutions.

JACQUES COURVOISIER, Professor, DD, born 1900 in Geneva. Since 1939 church historian at the University of Geneva.

SUSANNE DRESS, youngest sister of Dietrich Bonhoeffer, born 1909 in Breslau, in 1929 married Licentiate Walter Dress, who has been a pastor in Berlin-Dahlem since 1938 and is also a professor of church history at the Berlin *Kirchliche Hochschule* (Church College).

OTTO DUDZUS, Pastor, born 1912 in Essen, met Bonhoeffer during his studies in 1933, 1937 in Finkenwalde. 1946–54 chaplain at the Berlin *Kirchliche Hochschule*, since then parish minister in Cologne.

FRITZ FIGUR, Superintendent, born 1904 in Berlin. Once pastor at the Berlin Segenskirche, now superintendent of the diocese Berlin-Oberspree, also President of the Provincial Synod of Berlin-Brandenburg.

# The Contributors

H. FISCHER-HÜLLSTRUNG, one-time camp doctor of the Flossenbürg concentration camp. Shortly before his death sent this brief report to W. D. Zimmermann, in a letter of 4th April 1955.

ADOLF FREUDENBERG, Pastor, Dr. jur., born 1894 in Weinheim-Bergstrasse, after quitting the foreign service in 1935 joined the Confessing Church which sent him, after theological studies and ordination, to London. There, and later in Geneva with the Ecumenical Council, he devoted himself to the Refugee Service. He lives in the refugee settlement of Bad Vilbel-Heilsberg, which he ran from 1947 until his retirement.

JOHANNES GOEBEL, Pastor, born 1910 in Danzig-Langfuhr, was a member of the first seminary course in 1935, in Zingst and Finkenwalde; has been the pastor of the St. Katharinenkirche in Brandenburg-Havel since 1948.

HELMUT GOLLWITZER, Professor, DD, born 1908 in Pappenheim. 1938–40 pastor in Berlin-Dahlem; in Russian prison camp till 1950. He was called to a Chair by the University of Bonn and since 1957 has been teaching at the Free University of West Berlin.

OSKAR HAMMELSBECK, Professor, D.PHIL., born 1899 in Elberfeld, in 1937 became the head of the Seminary for Catechists of the Confessing Church in Berlin, in 1946 became professor and rector at the *Pädagogische Akademie* (Teachers' Training College) in Wuppertal, where he now lives in retirement.

FRANZ HILDEBRANDT, Professor, DD, a friend of Bonhoeffer's since their student years at Berlin University, became Niemöller's colleague in Berlin-Dahlem and left Germany for good in 1937; worked as a pastor from 1939–51 (besides doing academic work) in Cambridge, then for two years in Edinburgh. Since 1953 he has lived in the United States as professor of theology at Drew University in Madison, New Jersey.

GERHARD JACOBI, DD, born 1891 in Bremen, called to the Berlin Gedächtniskirche as a pastor in 1930, from 1933–9 President of the Confessing Church in Berlin, became General Superintendent of Berlin in 1945, has been Bishop of Oldenburg since 1954.

HANS-WERNER JENSEN, Pastor, Dr., born 1912 in Kiel, was in Bonhoeffer's Preachers' Seminary at Gross-Schlönwitz in 1938–9, was ordained in the Confessing Church in Berlin. Called to the Administrative Office of the *EKD* (Evangelical Church of Germany) in 1945 as a theological adviser, afterwards returning to parish work; since 1951 pastor at the St. Michaelskirche in Kiel.

# The Contributors

WERNER KOCH, Pastor, born 1910 in Bielefeld, joined the second Finken-walde seminary course in 1935, arrested in 1936 shortly before his ordination and imprisoned in the concentration camp of Sachsenhausen till 1938. Up to 1946 camp chaplain as a prisoner of war of the British Army; in 1947 called to a Berlin congregation, and after five years to Espelkamp; since 1955 parish minister in Netphen-Sieg.

FERENC LEHEL, Pastor, coming from Sopron, studied in Basle and Berlin where he was Bonhoeffer's student in 1932-3. Pastor in a con-gregation of poor agricultural workers of the Lutheran Church in Hungary, where he founded a co-operative self-aid for the villagers who were practically still serfs. Being a conscientious objector during the war, he was called up into the *Arbeitsdienst* (Labour Service). Since 1952 he has looked after a city congregation in Szombathely, and since 1963 has been an independent member of the Hungarian parliament.

PAUL LEHMANN, Professor, DD, born 1906. Religious editor of the West-minster Press in the U.S.A. 1946-7. Has held professorships at Prince-ton Theological Seminary, the Harvard Divinity School and, since 1963, at Union Theological Seminary, New York. After the war, he became especially interested in the problem of German rehabilitation and wrote *Re-educating Germany*.

SABINE LEIBHOLZ, Dietrich Bonhoeffer's twin sister, born 1906 in Breslau, married Gerhard Leibholz, later professor for civil law, in 1926. After some years at the universities of Greifswald and Göttingen she emigrated with her two daughters and her husband, who was en-dangered by persecution, to England and found refuge in London and Oxford. Since 1956 she has lived in Karlsruhe where her husband is a judge at the *Bundesverfassungsgericht* (Federal Constitutional Assize).

HENRY SMITH LEIPER, Pastor, DD, born 1891 in Belmont, New Jersey, until 1929 missionary in China; then entirely devoted himself to the Ecumenical Movement, as ecumenical secretary of the Federal Council of Churches in the United States, and since 1938 as Associate General Secretary of the Ecumenical Council (in process of formation). He lives in Leonia, New Jersey.

GOTTFRIED MALTUSCH, Pastor, born 1911 in Berlin, belonged to the Confessing Church from the beginning, one of the leaders of its youth work in Berlin. Took part in Bonhoeffer's Team Curacy in Köslin. Called to Oldenburg as pastor of the *Land* Youth Work in 1945; has been working for the Home Mission in Hanover since 1954 and has directed its central administration since 1957.

# The Contributors

REINHOLD NIEBUHR, Professor, DD, born 1892. 1915–28 pastor in Detroit, has won world-wide reputation as a theologian with social concerns and professor at Union Theological Seminary in New York. His contribution to this volume is taken from a letter written to W. D. Zimmermann on 28th December 1955.

WILHELM NIESEL, Professor, DD, born 1903 in Berlin, went to school at the Friedrichs-Werder Gymnasium, studied theology from 1922 in Berlin, Tübingen and Göttingen, did research on Calvin in Switzerland from 1926 to 1928, worked after that at the Elberfeld Preachers' Seminary. Called to Berlin in 1934 to become a member of the Council of the Evangelical Church of the Old Prussian Union, thus holding a place of authority within the Confessing Church. In 1946 he became the pastor of the Reformed congregation in Schöller and a professor at the Church College in Wuppertal. He is a member of the Council of the EKD (Evangelical Church of Germany); moderator of the Reformed Alliance and since 1964 President of the Reformed World Alliance.

HARALD POELCHAU, Pastor, Dr., born 1903 in Potsdam, commenced his theological studies in 1922, which brought him in close contact with Paul Tillich, under whose guidance he received his Licentiate of Theology. From 1933 pastor in Tegel prison where he helped innumerable victims of the Third Reich. He belonged to the Kreisau group. In 1945 he assisted Eugen Gerstenmaier in founding the *Evangelische Hilfswerk* ('Christian Aid'); for three years worked in the ministry of justice in the Soviet zone of Germany trying to bring about reforms in criminal procedures, and since 1951 has directed the church's *Sozialpfarramt* (industrial chaplaincy) in Berlin.

GERHARD VON RAD, Professor, DD, born 1901 in Nuremberg; in 1930 lecturer at Leipzig University, in 1934 professor of Old Testament Language and Literature in Jena, in 1945 at Göttingen University and since 1949 at Heidelberg University.

JULIUS RIEGER, Superintendent, Dr., born 1901 in Berlin, studied theology in Berlin, Bethel and Berne, was inspector of studies at the Preacher's Seminary at Naumberg/Queis. In 1930 became the pastor of the German Lutheran St. George's Church in London, a post which he held for twenty-three years. Since 1953 he has been superintendent in Berlin-Schöneberg. His recollections contained in this volume are part of a more substantial book to be published by Lettner Verlag, Berlin.

# The Contributors

RICHARD ROTHER, born in Berlin in 1918, was one of Dietrich Bonhoeffer's confirmands and from 1932 to 1935 worked in the law office of Dr. Klaus Bonhoeffer. From 1935 to 1943 he worked in an industrial plant of Berlin, latterly as manager of its accountancy office. At the end of 1943 he was conscripted into the Army. Since 1960 he has lived in Frankfurt/Main where he works for a Swiss industrial firm as manager of the accountancy department.

WILHELM ROTT, Superintendent, born 1908 in Düsseldorf, assisted Bonhoeffer from 1935-7 in Finkenwalde as inspector of studies; after that called to the Provisional Church Government in Berlin. Served in the *Abwehr*, interned after the war; in 1946 became a parish minister in Koblenz where he has been a superintendent since 1959.

OTTO SALOMON, Dr., born 1889 in Frankfurt/Main; in 1920 founded, with Georg Flemmig, the Brotherhood of the Open Ring, became known, in the following years, under the name of Otto Bruder, mainly by his plays for laymen, was the head of the Christian Kaiser Verlag (Publishing House) until 1938 where he helped to disseminate the writings of the Confessing Church. Threatened by the persecution of the Jews, he had to emigrate to Switzerland where he devoted himself to literary works and mainly, during the war, to the care of prisoners of war. A new creative era began for him when he became head of the Zwingli-Verlag alongside which he founded the Flamberg-Verlag. He lives in Zollikon near Zürich.

FABIAN VON SCHLABRENDORFF, Lawyer, born 1907 in Halle-Saale, went to school in Detmold, studied law, political economy and political science in Halle and Berlin. When an officer at the Russian front, he and his friend Colonel von Tresckow made an attempt to assassinate Hitler in 1943. After the 20th July he was arrested and, like Bonhoeffer, sent to the Flossenbürg concentration camp before the war ended. After the war he returned to his profession and now lives in Wiesbaden.

ALBRECHT SCHÖNHERR, General Superintendent, born 1911 in Katscher (Upper Silesia), joined the first Finkenwalde seminary course in 1935, was sent to Greifswald in 1936 by the Confessing Church, and a year later as a pastor to Brüssow. In 1946 he took over a parish in Brandenburg-Havel and in 1951 became the head of the Preachers' Seminary there. In 1963 he took on the newly founded post of General Superintendent of the Kurmark, in Eberswalde.

WOLFGANG SCHRADER, Pastor, born 1910 in Königsberg, took part in the first seminary course in Zingst and Finkenwalde, became a pastor in Kuhz-Uckermark, later in Stuttgart and finally in Berlin where he lives in retirement owing to ill health.

# The Contributors

HELLMUT TRAUB, Pastor, born 1904 in Dortmund, studied law and theology in Munich, Berlin, Tübingen, Bonn; concentration camp at Dachau; pastor in Fürstenwalde and Potsdam; seminary of the Confessing Church in Pomerania; pastor in Glinde, Volksdorf, Stuttgart (Reformed congregation).

WILLEM A. VISSER'T HOOFT, Dr., born 1900 in Haarlem, took his doctorate at the University of Leiden and was called by John Mott to Geneva to be secretary of the World Alliance of the YMCA. In 1931 he became the General Secretary of the World's Student Christian Federation. From 1938 he was general secretary of the World Council of Churches (in process of formation) and during the war enjoyed the full confidence of Bonhoeffer. On the final establishment of the World Council in 1948 he was confirmed afresh in his office and has remained the leading representative of the ecumenical movement. His contribution to this volume is part of a paper which he read in the Berlin *Kongresshalle* on 9th April 1965. The complete paper has been published in no. 5 of the *Berliner Reden* by Lettner Verlag Berlin, under the title: 'Dietrich Bonhoeffer 1945–65, by W. A. Visser't Hooft and Günter Jacob'.

LAWRENCE B. WHITBURN, born 1902, after school and apprenticeship spent the years 1923–30 in Germany; to that time he owes his connection with the Lutheran Church and his wife, who came from East Prussia. From 1930 to 1933 he lived in Forest Hill where he met Bonhoeffer. Since 1951 he has been departmental head of a metal factory in Manchester, also secretary and organist at the Martin Luther Church there.

WOLF-DIETER ZIMMERMANN, *Konsistorialrat* (Consistory councillor), born 1911 in Barmen, met Bonhoeffer in 1932 at Berlin University and came to Finkenwalde in 1936. Was a pastor in Berlin-Tegel after 1945 and with a group of young theologians founded the journal *Unterwegs*, where Bonhoeffer's posthumous works were first published. In 1954 he was nominated Broadcasting Commissioner for the Evangelical Church in Berlin-Brandenburg and head of the Evangelical Radio Service in Berlin.